HerStory Breaking Through Darkness

A MEMOIR

MERCEDES JOHNSON

Dedication

TO ALL THE trials, tests, pain, hurt, rejection, etc., that I had to endure in life. I believe it was all the downfalls, tears, and pain that has made me the person I am today. So God I thank you for allowing me to experience *everything* I have experienced. Thank you.

To my family, you all are the best. You all have witnessed my life go from darkness to light, sorrow to joy, tears to laughter and bondage to freedom. Though it took you all some time to understand the transition in my life, I thank you all from the bottom of my heart for receiving me, loving me and allowing my life/light lead you all to developing a personal relationship with the LORD. I love you all.

To my spiritual mother/ mentor Tanya Jameson. God bless you. I thank our Father for placing you in my life. I thank you for taking the time with me to pray with and for me. You have taught me Biblical principles, how to develop a relationship with God and what it means to have an intimate relationship with our Lord Jesus Christ. I truly thank you and I pray that our heavenly Father bless you abundantly. I love you.

Lastly, I thank my Abba Father for the spirit of Adoption and breaking the spirit of rejection off my mind, soul and spirit. Thank you Abba.

Note from Author

All the names in this book have been changed for privacy and dignity of the people. Lastly, this book is based on a child's life between the ages of four to nine years of age.

Contents

Preface

Part I   Ground Breaker

     1   Shovel to the Ground

     2   Dig Deep

     3   The Deeper the Seed, the Deeper the Dig

     4   The System of Bondage

     5   Invasion of Poverty

Part II   Everything Isn't as Pretty on the Outside

     1   The Sugar Isn't Always Sweet

     2   Material Isn't Enough I Need Love

     3   Bigger Than Us

HERSTORY BREAKING THROUGH DARKNESS

		4	Tried in the Fire
Part	III		Wolves in Sheep Clothing
		1	Smooth Operator
		2	Same Tune Different Step
		3	One Plus One Equals One
		4	When Sweetness Turns to Bitterness
Part	IV		THE UNFORGETTABLE
		1	The Unforgettable
		2	The Reality of the Unforgettable
		3	Now Behold the Unforgettable
		4	Death, Burial, Goodbye
		5	RESULTS
Part V			CONCLUDE

Conclusion

Prayer/ Prophetic Word/Release

Preface
~ ~ ~ ~

SOMETIMES, PAIN RUNS so deep to the point it leave you thinking if there would ever be an end. You sit and wonder why? Why it had to be you who endured the battles and whips of the unbearable pains of distress, rejection, depression, neglect, molestation and suicidal thoughts.

Yes. You know and understand that everyone has a story- a story to be shared and heard from the ears and hearts of many who are still or have been tortured from the pains of their upbringing. But this pain: My pain. Her story. My story is different from your story. My levels and depths of pain are different from yours.

See, pain knows no gender, color or age. Pain comes from a form of hurt. There are many levels of pain,

HERSTORY BREAKING THROUGH DARKNESS

and within the different levels, each one births out characteristics that entraps the mind of the individual. When the mind falls under subjection to the character of the pain, it eventually transforms the person's identity.

When one endures pain time after time during childhood, his or her God-given identity undergoes attack and eventually is stripped from him of her before her or she steps into adulthood. The depths of pain are real. It can create identity crises due to the many masks a person wears, with the attempt to cover up the pains, especially childhood pains and traumas.

The worst type of pain a person can encounter is the pain and hurt of their childhood. These are the worst and the most painful ones that we all try to run away from. Our childhood pains and wounds is what mold us into the person we become in our teenage and adult years. And it is up to us to face and deal with them.

I know it hurts. Just the thought of the day when

you first was raped or molested brings back the fear, hurt and pain you felt as a child. It hurt. I get it. I know it does. No, It wasn't your fault that your mother was a crackhead and your father was a pimp who wanted nothing to do with you. I understand you didn't ask to be born, and the very thought of it brings an uproar of anger within you. I truly understand, but when? When are you going to stop allowing the secrets of your past dictate your present and your future? I understand some things feel or seem more shameful than others. You promised to take it to the grave with you. It's too shameful. You think about what people will say if they knew you were a homosexual or a lesbian. What would they think if they knew you struggled with pornography? What will they say? What will they do? Just the thought of someone finding out sends trembles down your spine along with cold sweats from the years of fear and hiding.

    The truth of the

HERSTORY BREAKING THROUGH DARKNESS

matter is that you didn't wake up and decide that you were going to be a homosexual, a lesbian, a child molester, a drug addict, or a prostitute. You didn't choose that title. Though a part of you has accepted it and has submitted to the mind of that lifestyle, your childhood pains still hunt you and torments you daily. And it is because of unhandled scars from your childhood that has molded you into the man or woman that you are today. These are seeds that have been planted.

You thought if you forgot about your father and uncles sneaking in your room every night to have their way with your nine-year-old body that it will all go away. You thought maybe if you blotted out the scenes of seeing your mother get beat every other night that it will all go away. But how wrong you were. They didn't go away. No matter how many times and how far you have tried to push them away they have not left you alone. The thoughts wouldn't flee. The nightmares wouldn't leave you be and not to

MERCEDES JOHNSON

mention the memories-The brutal memories, that has left a deadly scar on your heart and soul still to this very day.

You might be sitting here reading this, thinking how can I say that I understand you. How can I say I understand your pain and what your past has done to you? I didn't have to walk in your shoes, your hurt, your pain and your lies everyday hoping that no one would ever find out. I don't know your story. I don't know your pain. You didn't ask for this. You didn't ask to be a whore, a pimp, a drug addict, a homosexual or a lesbian. You didn't. You didn't ask for it, but this was the hand that was dealt to you and you're playing it the best way you know how.

Yes, you are surely right. I haven't had to walk in your exact shoes, but I need you to listen; there's always somebody's story that is worse than yours. It doesn't mean that what you have been through does not serve a purpose because it does. Though you have experienced some form of hurt and pain during

HERSTORY BREAKING THROUGH DARKNESS

your upbringing, it does not limit you as a person. If anything, it ought to make you stronger. There's healing in our brokenness. Though you might be broken as of right now, remember in the midst of your brokenness, you can be healed and strengthened.

I would like to introduce to you all a young lady by the name of Jada Rose. I want you all to sit back, fasten your seat belt, put your helmet on, and enjoy the bumpy ride of the life of Ms. Jada Rose. This is her story breaking through darkness.

MERCEDES JOHNSON

GROUND BREAKER

1
Shovel to The Ground
~ ~ ~ ~

"NO, NO, NO!" screaming at the top of her lungs, nine-year-old Jada lies in her bed with her body soaked in perspiration. This was her fifth time out the week where her sleep has been viciously interrupted by horrifying nightmares.

Her small frail body shook violently. She remained in bed wishing the images and voices would leave. She just wanted to be left alone. But she knew all too well that the nightmares wouldn't leave her alone or the voices that came along with them. This has become a part of her life. She thought of ways to incorporate the nightmares into her daily life. These nightmares have been with Jada for as long as she knew. Though they have been with her, she dared not to tell anyone.

I will never tell anyone. Never. I can't, Jada wrestled with these thoughts on an everyday basis.

She knew she couldn't tell anyone what she was dealing with. She had sworn in secrecy to herself that she would never tell anyone. Not ever. If she had to take this secret to the grave with her, so be it. Stubbornness sat on the door of her heart.

What young Jada didn't know was that even though she promised herself never to talk about it or think about it, the memories was never going to leave her. She was tortured mentally daily and held as a prisoner by her own childhood secrets.

What would people

HERSTORY BREAKING THROUGH DARKNESS

say or think if I told them? Just the thought of exposing herself made her skin crawl. She repeatedly told herself that it was her fault. She was the blame. It wouldn't matter if she said anything or not because she was the reason why things happened the way they did.

Through clenched teeth and tears, Jada sat up in the middle of her bed and cried out, "it was my fault. I made him do it. I must have done something for him to do what he done to me. He wasn't in the wrong. I'm the whore. I was too fast. It was I. I'm the blame. Not him." Anguish was all over her face. Her tears poured hastily down her face as she writhed her shaking hands.

****

My name is Jada Rose, and I was born on the Southside of Chicago in Robert Taylor housing projects. My mother and father were young teenagers when they gave birth to me. I was born out of wedlock, meaning when Mama and Daddy had me, they weren't married.

MERCEDES JOHNSON

I don't remember a lot about Daddy during my childhood. However, there is one thing that I do remember and that is that Daddy was taken to prison when I was four years old. Daddy's absence didn't affect me. Well, at least, I didn't think it did. Though I knew who my father was, I still didn't know him. Daddy and I didn't share a father and daughter relationship. There were no memories of him and I, and to add, there were no memories of him that sparked any hope of seeing him again.

I didn't realize the absence of Daddy until I got older. After Daddy went to prison, I watched Mama drown herself in alcohol. It is a strong possibility that Mama drank before Daddy came and left the picture, but I remember noticing and being able to comprehend Mama's drinking habit when Daddy went to prison.

I watched Mama drown in alcohol, and it wasn't just her, but also the people she surrounded with. I lived in an environment where

HERSTORY BREAKING THROUGH DARKNESS

drinking, smoking, partying, carrying guns, and fighting were normal. That was all I saw, and at the time, that was all I knew.

Mama was young when she had me; she was seventeen and Daddy was sixteen. She was still a child herself. Though she was young, Mama was pretty straightforward, and she made sure I didn't step out of line. She taught me a lot of mannerism. When talking to her and other adults I was told to say, "Yes, ma'am" and "No, ma'am."

Mama didn't play. And I didn't want to cross the line with her. I tried to stay on my best behavioral when I was around her.

I was indeed a mama's girl. I loved mama. She was all I knew.

Though I was young and innocent, I wasn't naïve to hurt and pain. Matter of fact, those two became my best friends at a young age. I was the only child so I did a lot of things by myself. I always wanted to be under Mama, but Mama was young, and she wanted to drink and party.

Mama always dropped me off to either a friend or family member's house. Sometimes, she'll leave me for a day, and sometimes, it will be days.

As a child, I could never understand why and how she could leave me at someone's house for days. I guess I couldn't understand because I never wanted to be away from Mama. I loved being around her, and I know that Mama felt the same way, but she was young and she too was still a child with grown-up responsibilities.

Mama and I were completely different. Mama always smiled; she was really friendly and greeted and embraced everyone. Mama had such a big heart, and she didn't like to see people mistreated. I, on the other hand, was a very shy, timid and a quiet child. It took time for me to warm up to people. I had my moments when I would talk and then there were times when I wouldn't say anything, and Mama hated it when I got in that mood. Whenever we were around her friends, I will hide behind her. I never really liked to talk. For some odd reason, I was scared. What was I scared of? I don't know. But I know I was very shy around Mama's friends.

You can imagine the depths of hurt and pain I felt when Mama would drop me off at people's houses. It was these moments when my little heart and soul was completely crushed. Whenever Mama and I would go to her friends' house, I would try to stay close to her. I would never want to play with the other kids. I just wanted to be with Mama mainly because I knew that if I turned my back, she was going to sneak out the door and leave me.

Mama didn't like it when I was under her around her friends. Mama would always remind me that I was not a grown up, and when grown people were talking, kids needed to leave the room. One of Mama's favorite lines of dismissing me was, "You do as I say and not as I do, now move around." All her friends would laugh and give her high fives. I knew better than to try to ignore her or pretend I didn't hear what she was saying. Mama established and enforced rules and understanding of respect real quick with me.

My little heart couldn't grasp mama's dismissal no matter how many times she did it. Every time felt like the first time, and my reactions remained the same. I would walk away with my chin touching my chest with tears falling down my face, wetting the front of my shirt. My feelings would be extremely hurt.

My little heart and feelings would be so crushed, and my feelings would take over my mind and have me thinking, *Mama doesn't love me. If she did she wouldn't treat me like she did.* This was my mental silent battle. "No matter what, I'll always love you mommy," I would say as I slowly walked away with my head still hanging down.

When I got inside

the kid's room of Mama's friend, I stayed near the door so I could hear Mama's voice and laughter. I didn't want her to leave me. I was aware of Mama's plans now. Every time she brought me to a friend or family member's house Mama would wait until I turned my back, then she would run out the door.

I would run to the door behind her banging on the closed door screaming, at the top of my lungs as if I was near death. I would lie in front of the door crying for Mama to come back for me. Mama's friend's kids would try to cheer me up and take my mind off the absence of Mama, but it wouldn't work. I knew if Mama decided to come back to get me the night she left, she was going to come back drunk.

This too became a norm for my life. Mama drank every day. She didn't drink just to get tipsy. No. Mama drank to get drunk. I abhorred this about mama. I hated it with everything in me. I wished and wanted Mama to stop drinking. I really wish she did. But from the looks of it alcohol appeared to be a part of Mama's life, just like pain and hurt became a part of my childhood life.

****

If I can go back to a specific event with Mama and her alcohol addiction, I will go back to when I was either six or seven years old, maybe even younger. I remember Mama held a party at our apartment. Our apartment was really crowded that night. All of Mama's friends were present, men and women. The music was blasting throughout the apartment. Aluminum pans were stacked on the kitchen counters with barbecue chicken, ribs, hamburgers, hot links, and everything else you can possibly think of. In Chicago, pulling out the grill and barbecuing was a daily thing to do regardless of the weather.

It wasn't a party if there wasn't barbecue, card playing, music, stepping and most of all alcohol and there

HERSTORY BREAKING THROUGH DARKNESS

was plenty of all five. Mama and her friends not only drank, but they drunk dark liquor and tall cans of beer. Mama really loved her beer especially Olde English 800 and white port and Kool-Aid.

  On this specific day, I wasn't allowed to come out of the room. The only time I was able to come out was if I had to use the restroom or retrieve food for myself. I obeyed Mama and stayed in the room watching VHS movies. As the day dragged into the wee hours of the night, one by one, Mama's friends began to stagger out the door. I don't remember the specific timing, but I remember Mama coming in the room with me falling sloppily on the bed. As soon as she hit the bed, she was instantly down for the count. Mama knew she could snore, especially when she was heavily intoxicated. Her snoring filled the room to the point it began to drown out the television.

  My little body was full of fierce anger. I hated when Mama drank, especially when she got drunk. I secretly developed a silent bitterness, anger and disgust toward Mama and her alcohol addiction.

    I tried turning the volume up on the television, but that didn't help. It seemed like every time I turned the volume up, Mama would snore louder. I finally gave up on watching television and turned it off. I looked over at Mama, and anger instantly took over. Everything in me wanted to grab her and shake her until her desire and addiction left her body. That's how much I hated it. Whenever Mama would start drinking, it was like she would turn into another person. She would talk really loud, cuss word after cuss word will come flying out of her mouth, and she would fight a lot. But underneath all of that, Mama had such a big heart. She loved people. She might have fought a lot, but Mama had a caring heart.

    As I sat there staring at her, my love for her quickly took over the anger and frustration I felt toward her. I crawled over to where

HERSTORY BREAKING THROUGH DARKNESS

Mama was lying, and I positioned myself up under her.

When Mama and I would spend time together, it was the best. We would watch movies together while lying up under one another. It was the best. She was the best.

I squirmed around for a while until I found a nice comfortable position under her. I lied there and listened to Mama's heavy breathing and snoring.

Mama must have had too much to drink because she was sleeping, and there were people still in the living room packing up to leave. I listened to the voices of the few people that were still present, and I noticed that it was family so I paid them no mind. My eyes were starting to get heavy, but for some reason, my body was extremely restless. I eventually zoned out listening to Mama's heavy breathing.

As I drifted off to sleep, I soon was knocked out of my sleep when I felt the side of my leg become warm and wet. I jumped out of the bed in a swift move and looked

MERCEDES JOHNSON

hastily at the sheets and saw that they too were wet.

This too wasn't new to me. Mama didn't always pee on herself when she was drunk, but I noticed when Mama got too drunk like this she would urinate on herself.

I was beyond tired of this. My rage came right back. I was furious. I hated this. It was times like this when I hated Mama. I resented her. I wished she would just stop drinking. I hated what it did to her. It brought such a separation between her and I. I felt like I was watching alcohol take Mama away from me. Instead of Mama and I being close, she ran to the bottle where she thought she could find peace. She only drowned herself in liquor, and by the end of the night, she was down in the bottom of the bottle, but her problems and pain still remained.

Whenever Mama was at home by herself drinking, she would usually turn off all the lights and listen to her old dusty songs like Lenny Williams; Switch; Isley Brothers; Earth, Wind & Fire, etc.

HERSTORY BREAKING THROUGH DARKNESS

Mama loved her oldies with her tall can of Ole English 800.

During these nights, I noticed Mama would sit up by herself, and some nights, she would stay up crying all night, drinking and listening to her oldies. Mama drank a lot and cried a lot when she was alone. Though I was young, I felt Mama's pain. I noticed and understood that Mama was hurt. I wanted to tell her that I understood. I felt her pain and she wasn't alone, but I knew better. "A child was to stay in a child's place," and that wasn't my place. So majority of these nights, I stayed quiet in my room leaning my ear on the door crying myself to sleep.

The door in my room that separated Mama and I symbolized Mama's heart. Whenever I placed my ear on the door and pressed it hard enough against it, I would hear the cries that she shed alone. I heard the hurt, pain and fear that I too was living with.

****

As I looked down at Mama sleeping, I knew I

couldn't leave her sleeping in her own urine. Even though everything in me wanted to, I knew I couldn't do Mama like that.

I left the room where Mama was sound asleep and went into the bathroom. I turned on the hot water, grabbed a clean white face towel and soap, and I made sure that the towel was soapy enough so I could clean the urine off of Mama.

When I walked out the bathroom and made my way into the room, what I saw scared me internally. I wanted to scream at the top of lungs and beat him to death. Murder was on my mind, and slowly began to take over me.

I walked in the room and saw Mama's male "friend" leaning over her. He wasn't just leaning over her, but he was kissing on her and forcefully trying to pull her pants down. At the sight of this, I felt my heart drop to the pit of my stomach and my throat instantly closed up. I don't know if it was fear or anger that paralyzed me, but I know whatever it was, it stopped me from moving. It was as if I was frozen. I tried opening my mouth, but no words came out. I tried moving, but I was paralyzed. I stood and watched as my burning hot tears fell from the wells of my eyes rubbing against my cheeks.

Mama was so drunk to the point that she didn't budge. She didn't move. She was just lying there snoring. One would've sworn that she must have been unconscious. I hated her. I hated him. I screamed on the inside, *How can you get this drunk that you don't feel this man trying to take advantage of you? Mom. Please get up. Get up. Get off of her. Leave my mom alone. Leave her alone*. It almost felt like someone had his or her hand over my mouth, and it prevented me from talking.

It felt like I was being forced to watch this. I was being tortured. Mama was helpless. She didn't move, and I couldn't help her. He continued to kiss on her. He forcefully pulled Mama shirt up, hastily pulling her breast from her bra and slobbered on them. In the midst of doing this he was still struggling to get Mama's pants down.

The struggle eventually ended and he got her pants half way down. I remember seeing the look on his face. How focused he was to get Mama's pants down and when he finally did, a smirk slithered across his face.

I don't know happened in that moment, but as he began to pull his pants down, it felt like the hand that was over my mouth was removed. The paralyzing feeling I felt soon left, but the anger. The anger and hatred tripled in my young heart. I was full of hate and anger; I wanted to kill him right then and there. But I couldn't.

Though I was full of anger, I couldn't move fast enough. As I proceeded toward him, my steps were stiff and very slow. I walked over to him and slowly said, "What are you doing?" His body jerked and stiffened up when he heard my voice. Without responding, he quickly pulled Mama's shirt down and climbed off of her.

HERSTORY BREAKING THROUGH DARKNESS

As he opened his mouth, he began to stutter, "I, I, I, was saying bye," he said as he stumbled past me out the room. I stood there for a moment looking at the door with murder and hate on my heart and mind, but when I directed my attention to Mama, it all vanished away. As I looked at Mama, all my hurt, pain and anger soon went away. I moved slowly toward her and gently took Mama's clothes off and wiped her off with the soapy towel that was now warm. As I wiped her, I couldn't help but cry. It pained me. Even when I was wiping her, Mama still didn't move. It was like she was dead or just completely lifeless.

When I got done, I wrapped Mama up in a clean sheet and placed a blanket over her. After moving her heavy stiff body to the other side of the bed out of her urine, I was beyond exhausted. But I couldn't sleep. I got in the bed next to Mama and held her. I silently made a vow to her, "I'll never let you go." I cried myself to sleep while the images played vividly in my head.

MERCEDES JOHNSON

I finally went to sleep with Mama in my arms and streaks of tears down my cheek.

I was awakened the next morning to Mama laughing with her boyfriend and my aunt. When I heard Mama's voice I was startled and woke up immediately. Mama was up talking about how much fun she had and how drunk she was. She mentioned how she urinated on herself.

I listened to Mama talk for a while before heading to the restroom. I was contemplating in my head the right time and way to express to Mama what happened when she was asleep. I didn't want to ruin everything, but the burden was too heavy on me, and I couldn't carry it on my own. I had to tell Mama what happened.

After I got myself together in the restroom, I joined Mama, her boyfriend and my aunt in the living room, and I sat with them at the table. I remember the feeling I felt as soon as I sat down. Disgust filled my being. I couldn't understand why Mama had to drink every day. I didn't understand. One thing I did understand was the hatred and disgust I felt whenever I saw her drink. I had pure hatred toward alcohol and people that indulged in it, especially those that drunk with Mama. I wished Mama had different friends. I wish she had friends who didn't drink, but everybody in the area we lived in were either alcoholics or drug addicts. Everybody had an alcoholic, heron or crack addict in their family. This way of living was normal, and no one tried to hide his or her addiction.

    As I sat at the table, Mama acknowledged me with her famous smile. I loved when Mama smiled. When she smiled, she showed all thirty-two of her teeth.

    Smiling back I said, "Hi mom." I couldn't help but to smile and giggle. Being around Mama, joy rose up from the inside of me. I wondered if she knew that behind my smile was a lot of built up hurt and anger? I had to tell

MERCEDES JOHNSON

Mama what happened. I couldn't take it anymore. I tried to push the images out of my mind, but they kept coming back more vivid. As I sat there, my stomach began to turn and twist. I just knew I was about to vomit. I had to tell her whether she was ready to hear it or not. Mama deserved to know.

As I began to build up my confidence mentally, Mama removed herself from the table and headed to the bedroom. That was my opportunity to tell her. I headed to the room where I found her getting dressed.

"Mom," I said in almost a whisper.

She turned around toward me. "Yeah."

I loved Mama more than she'll ever know or understand. "Mom, yesterday, when you were in the room sleeping, I walked in the room and your friend Curtis was on top of you, trying to take your clothes and stuff." The words came out almost like vomit. They spilled out my mouth so fast that I did not

HERSTORY BREAKING THROUGH DARKNESS

take a breath. The look on Mama's face struck a pain in the pit of my stomach that traveled to the right side of my body.

From the look on Mama's face, I knew she was hurt. I wish had I never said anything. I didn't mean to hurt her. I loved her. I just wanted Mama to know.

My body was stricken with pain. I stood before her with my head held down in silence. Mama remained silent for what felt like minutes. Without saying a word, she walked past me and headed out the room. As soon as she left the room, I heard Mama, her boyfriend and sister exchanging words.

"Jada, why did you wait to say something? You know if you would've said something last night, dude wouldn't have walked up out of here." Mama's boyfriend came in the room questioning me.

Hunching my shoulders, "I don't know," I responded with my head down. There was a dead silence

MERCEDES JOHNSON

that filled the room. I slowly lifted my head up just enough to where I could see Mama's boyfriend facial expression. "I was scared." With that being said, I walked out the room.

No later than ten minutes, Mama, her boyfriend, and sister marched out the door and headed to the liquor store where Mama's friend Curtis worked. As they all began to leave, I listened from my room Mama talking about what she was going to do to him.

When Mama spoke like this, fear came over me because I knew Mama was a woman of her words. To be as young as I were, I have seen plenty of fights. In the projects, Mama was known for her fighting. She fought a lot. Mama had a sweet heart. Her smile alone was radiant and beyond beautiful, but underneath the smile, Mama must have had a lot of anger because everywhere she went, she fought. I personally don't believe Mama enjoyed fighting as much as she did, but growing up on the south side in the projects of Chicago, every one was a

HERSTORY BREAKING THROUGH DARKNESS

fighter.

The principle of fighting in the projects was whomever you fought, that person was considered your enemy, and depending on the level of tension and beef you two had, it was guaranteed that every time ya'll saw one another, there was going to be a fight. I learned this principle and rule from Mama.

Mama was a woman of her words. Whenever she said she was going to do something, you could count on her doing just that. The fact that I knew Mama well enough, I knew that if Curtis admitted to trying to have sex with her without her permission, it was going to be a fight. See, Mama wasn't the type that needed people to help her fight; she fought by herself with or without help. She didn't look for people to have her back. She took care of her own. Another thing that I knew about Mama was that she didn't have a problem fighting men.

I witnessed mama fistfight a lot of her boyfriends.

MERCEDES JOHNSON

There was a particular day I don't think I will ever forget. I believe I was either five or six. Mama had this boyfriend name Marcus; I would assume that she loved him because they fought so much, and she never left him. I never understood that, but I guess I was too young to try to understand their relationship.

This particular day was different from any other fight Mama and Marcus had throughout their relationship. I remember it was during the winter and the snow was piled up to our knees. Mama and I struggled through the knee-high snow and the bitter wind that roughly brushed across our naked face.

This day, Mama and I spent the afternoon and evening at her sister's house, my aunt. Mama and everyone there played spades on my aunt's long glass table. It was a beautiful table. Aunt took turns playing her hand of spades and frying chicken wings. There wasn't a lot of people there, but enough to have

HERSTORY BREAKING THROUGH DARKNESS

the music blasting Mary J Blige's album *My Life*. Auntie was a really big fan of Mary J. Blige. Conversation mixed with cuss words and laughter filled the apartment. Twelve packs of Budweiser and Olde English 800 were going around along with the conversations.

    We stayed there until the streetlights went out. By the time we left, Mama was good and drunk.

    "Jada!" Mama yelled toward the back room with a slur in her voice for me.

    "Yes, ma'am," I replied.

    "Grab your stuff, we are about to go," Mama said while, staggering and rushing to the restroom.

    I said my goodbyes to my cousins and met Mama in the living room with my coat and hat on. It took us longer than usual to get to our housing projects. Auntie lived on Forty-fifth and State Street, and Mama and I lived in 5100 Carter buildings, which was a little distance between our buildings. It usually took no longer than thirty minutes

MERCEDES JOHNSON

between our apartments, but this night, it took a lot longer. Mama staggered through the snow. She was really drunk. I knew Mama's boyfriend hated when she got this drunk. They usually got into fights on days like these.

We finally made it to our apartment, and when we got there, Marcus wasn't home, and that was a big mistake in Mama's eyes, especially since she was drunk. His absence sparked a fire within her that I knew wasn't going to be easy to put out. Personally, I was happy that Marcus wasn't there, but I knew Mama wasn't, and it showed all over her face. She grabbed her pack of Newport 100's, lit one and began bickering. From the way she was talking, Mama assumed that Marcus should've been home, and the fact that he wasn't, Mama believed he was cheating.

Marcus was a young drug dealer. It wasn't a surprise to me that he sold drugs because everybody sold, used or did both. Whenever Marcus wasn't home at the time Mama thought he

HERSTORY BREAKING THROUGH DARKNESS

should've been home, she would always say that he wasn't out all night serving. I figured if Mama knew that Marcus was out messing around with other women, she would leave him, but I guess it wasn't that simple or easy.

    The moment Marcus walked through the door the battle was on instantly. Mama didn't even allow him to get in the house all the way before she began to cussing him out and questioning him about his whereabouts. Mama quickly began to flood him with question after question. She didn't even allow him to thoroughly her. I guess his answers weren't satisfying because the moment he opened his mouth to answer, she immediately shut down everything he had to say. In situations like these, the liquor didn't make matters any better because it was no longer Mama talking but it was the liquor leading and guiding Mama's words. She wouldn't be quiet. After a while, Marcus didn't remain silent. He lost his cool, and when he lost his cool it caused that fire that was in Mama to flare out of control. Mama felt like he had no reason to be mad because he was the one out messing around, but Marcus wasn't trying to hear none of that. He was tired of Mama following him around, calling him out his name, and hitting him upside his head.

It was as if he transformed into someone else because out of nowhere, the name-calling began for him. I hated when he called Mama out her name. He called her all type of drunks. I knew his words hurt Mama because they would hurt me. I hated him. I wanted Mama to break up with him and be done with him so it could be just her and me without the violence and hurt.

It was obvious that Mama couldn't handle the name-calling from him because she started hitting him upside his head with her fist. As soon as I heard things crashing on the floor and against walls, I ran into the living room and witnessed Marcus having Mama pinned up against the wall with his hands around her neck. Mama was squirming around on the wall while trying to grab hold of his hands.

"I'll kill you. I'll kill you. You better stop playing with me, man," Mama's boyfriend repeatedly yelled these words while looking her square in her face. He slowly began to loosen his grip from around Mama neck. That was his first and last mistake. Mama didn't go down easily, and she didn't give up easily especially when it came to fighting. Mama wasn't done. As soon as he let her go, her fists one following after the other landed right in his face. She was moving so fast that it shocked Marcus and I. It was as if she got her second wind back because she was hitting him with some smooth combos and uppercuts.

Marcus was trying his best to grab her hands, but she was moving too fast. Mama kept punching him in his face until he somehow ducked down and grabbed her by her waist, picked her up, and slammed her on the floor.

I watched all this from the corner. Mama and

MERCEDES JOHNSON

Marcus looked like cats and dog the way they were fighting. In that moment, I said to myself if love makes a person do this, then I don't want it. Right then and there, I made a promise to myself that I hated all men, and I didn't want to be in a relationship because they all hurt.

Mama and Marcus wrestled on the floor until he found his way on top of her. I don't know if Mama became fearful when he was positioned over her, but I knew as soon as he got on top of her, she quickly lifted her upper body and grabbed hold of the side of his face with her teeth.

"Oooooooooouch," he yelped out loud.

The way Mama had her jaws locked; you would've sworn she was a pit bull. Marcus violently began punching mama wildly until she released her lock from the side of his face. When she let the side of his face go, Marcus grabbed her by her shirt and began dragging her across the floor toward the door. He was furious.

HERSTORY BREAKING THROUGH DARKNESS

I finally came out of hiding and ran up behind him; pounding on his back with my small bald-up fist as fast as I could while yelling, "Get off my mommy." My tears profusely fell from the wells of my eyes. "Leave her alone. Leave her alone," I cried out.

Quickly with one hand, he pushed me onto the floor. Before I knew it, I was right back on my feet so fast it seemed as if he never pushed me. When I got up, I was beyond angry- angrier than I was before. I jumped on top of Mama and wrapped my arms around her. With one swift move, he unlocked the door and slung Mama and I out of our apartment, slammed the door and locked it.

Mama stayed on the cold freezing ground, banging heavily on the door while weeping loudly. No matter how hard and long Mama banged on the door screaming for Marcus to open it, he never did.

This night, I remember Mama wrapping me up in her arms while I remained on top of her. I remember feeling her hot tears fall from her eyes down her cheek unto my forehead. I couldn't bear looking at Mama crying. I loved her. Whenever I saw Mama cry from the hands of others, anger and hate rose up in me. I hated to see Mama cry. Though majority of the times, she would cry to herself, but when she did cry in front of me, it was always by the hands of a man and sometimes the words of family members.

Just as much as Mama didn't like crying in front of me, I didn't like crying in front of her. We both had to be strong for one another. But this night was different. Mama and I held each other and cried silently in each other's arms. I remember I hid my face in Mama's bosom and wept silently, soaking the front of her shirt with my tears.

****

When Mama, her boyfriend, and sister departed, I frantically paced back and forth throughout our two-bedroom apartment waiting impatiently upon their arrival. As I paced back and forth, so many different scenes flashed in my mind. I pictured Mama stabbing him, cutting him, picking up a bottle and hitting him across his head or simply going toe to toe with him. Whichever one it was going to be, it had me in a nervous wreck. I didn't know why I was so nervous, but I guess I wondered about mostly was if he was going to tell the truth or deny it.

The slamming of the front door and the voices of Mama, her boyfriend and my aunt instantly brought me out of my train of thought. I guess it didn't go as bad as I thought because Mama came back with them.

"Jada," Mama called for me with a loud voice.

I made my way to her with one swift move. "Yes ma'am," I responded with nervousness in my voice and fear creeping up my spine.

I was what some might say scared of Mama. When I was in Mama's good grace, there was no sight of fear in my bone, but when Mama was mad, it was a different story. See, she didn't have to be mad at me in particular, but whenever she was mad, sad, depressed or any other emotion besides happy, fear would rise up from the inside of me and take over me.

Mama knew I was scared of her and she hated it, but I couldn't hide it or pretend that I wasn't. Whenever Mama would raise her hand or arms to reach for something, I would flinch. My hands will quickly fly up, and I will cover my face. Sometimes, I will flinch so hard that I will fall on the floor. I had a fear toward Mama that I didn't understand. Only thing I understood was that it was there and it was shown visibly. Mama hated it. She couldn't stand it. Every time I flinched, she would yell at me. Mama yelled at me no matter if we were in front of people or by ourselves. I would feel embarrassed, but I never thought once to tell Mama that she was embarrassing me. Heck no. Voicing my opinion was like cussing at her or another adult, and Mama didn't play those types of games.

I never wanted to be scare of Mama, but the fear that I had toward her was a part of me. I loved Mama so much, but within all my loving, I also feared her to the core of me. I wished I didn't fear her for the most part; I wished that it wasn't visible.

I remember there were times when people would tell Mama that I was scared of her and they would say things that referred to her way of disciplining me. Mama would respond in defense and say that she wasn't beating me and that I wasn't scared of her. One day, it got to the point that Mama called me from my room in front of everyone and asked me if I was scared of her. I wasn't sure if it was a trick question or what. Deep down in my heart, I knew that I was afraid of Mama. The type of fear that I had I don't think it was normal. I believe it was far deeper than my comprehension as a child.

MERCEDES JOHNSON

I remember that evening, I looked around at all of Mama's friends sitting around, drinking their tall cans of Olde English 800 then I looked back at Mama. It felt like all eyes were on me. I knew the truth in my heart, but I knew I had better have said other words than, "yes, Mama, I'm scared of you." After looking at Mama's friends then at Mama then back to them, I responded in my innocent voice, "No ma'am, I'm not scared of you, Mom." After saying those words, it felt like a lump as big as a log was in my throat. "Yes she is. Jada lying. She scared to even answer the question. That baby is scared of you," my cousin Raven, who was Dad's cousin, yelled out. I headed back to my room quickly before anything flared. I knew that it wasn't my cousin that was doing all the talking, but it was the beer that was talking for her. In environments like these, I knew the best thing for me to do was to dismiss myself and do it quickly.

When fear entered

HERSTORY BREAKING THROUGH DARKNESS

my life, I developed terrible speech impairment. I began to stutter badly. This too irked Mama's nerves. She thought that she could beat and threaten it out of me. But to both of our surprise, it only grew worse. As strange as this may sound, but I only would stutter as bad as I would was when I was around Mama. Let's get this understood, when I say it only came out around Mama, those were the times when Mama would be mad at me, and I knew that I was about to get punished. Before Mama would discipline me or punish me, she would take her time and ask me questions leading up to her whooping me. I never understood this process because at the end of the conversation, Mama always got angrier and my whooping would be worse. However, it was times like these or when Mama wasn't in a good mood when out of nowhere, I would try to answer Mama questions, and I would feel something grab hold of my tongue. I would try time after time to get my words out, but nothing will come out. There were times when I would

MERCEDES JOHNSON

stand before Mama crying because it would hurt while I fought to get my words out. Once my words would finally come out, it felt like something pushed them out roughly and violently. It was a very tiring process.

Mama hated when I stuttered. I believe I hated it more than she did. She didn't have to struggle and fight something she didn't see just to get a word out, and then go through the process all over again to get other words out. Mama didn't know this battle I went through just to talk. All she knew that, out of nowhere, I developed a habit of stuttering. She hated it, and I had better get it together before she did. She would threaten me and say all mean things to me whenever I would stutter. She would say things like, "Hurry up, get it out". She would go from saying encouraging things to, "don't nobody got all day for this, Jada, get it before I do it for you," or "Hurry up, get it out with your slow self." I didn't know which one hurt more-the invisible battle or Mama's hurtful words.

HERSTORY BREAKING THROUGH DARKNESS

I hated that I stuttered. I hated it even more because I knew Mama did as well. I tried to go out of my way to please her. All I ever wanted was for Mama to love me and accepted me.

****

When I made my way to the living room where Mama, her boyfriend and my aunt were sitting at the living room table, I stood silently next to her. "Yes, ma'am," I replied again to her.

Mama and her company were talking about what happened when they approached Mama's friend Curtis and how he denied everything and said that I was lying.

I wasn't lying. I wanted to yell out to Mama and tell her that I wasn't lying. What I saw was real and that he was the one that was lying. I couldn't verbally tell mama that Curtis was lying because Mama taught me to never call an adult a liar.

I remained silent on the outside, but on the inside, I

was furious. I wanted him dead. I felt like he was turning Mama against me. It wasn't fair. It wasn't fair. It wasn't fair.

"Jada, Jada, Jada," Mama was calling my name bringing me back to reality.

"Yes ma'am. I'm sorry, Mom."

"Did you hear me?"

"No ma'am. Sorry, Mom."

"Oh, I was saying I went to his job, and I told him what you told me, and he promised that he didn't do that and how you was lying."

My hurt busted out of me when Mama said that he said I was lying. It was as if I was hearing her call me a liar. "Mom, I promise I'm not lying, Mom. He was in the room on top of you."

"I believe you. See, he thought he was slick. I know that he liked me, but he knew that I was never going to give him none not even on his good day and my bad day. Only punks try to do stuff like that. You see how he tried to wait until I got drunk to try to pull something like that though?"

    I didn't know if Mama was asking me a question or if she was just talking. I wasn't sure if I should respond or not. I learned my lesson speaking when not spoken to. I didn't want to make Mama upset, and I didn't want to get embarrassed. So I remained silent until Mama dismissed me. Mama's favorite phrase she used when she was dismissing me was, "Do as I say and not as I do now move around." But she didn't say that; she grabbed me and hugged me for what felt like minutes.

    "I love you," Mama said while still holding me.

    "I love you too, Mom."

    I couldn't hold back my smile. Mama began playfully biting my cheeks. I tried squirming out of her hold. She locked her legs around my small body. This went on for a couple of minutes until Mama unlocked her legs from around me. Before releasing me, she gave me a wet sloppy kiss on both of my cheeks.

"Mom," I laughed while wiping my face swiftly.

She smiled at me then turned her attention back to the adults. That was the indication that grown folks were talking. Kids needed to be out of grown folks' mouth and conversation. If a child tried to stay under their parent(s) when company was around, that child was considered "too grown." Mama didn't play that. She didn't tolerate a child that acted too grown or a smart-mouth child. Mama raised me with respect for adults.

2
Dig Deep
~ ~ ~ ~

NEVER SHOULD A child have had to be exposed to so much abuse at a young age. However, I guess as people say, hurt and pain has no color, gender and in my situation it had no age. I wish someone would have taught or told Mama that, but how could I blame her, she was young herself. I loved Mama because she did her best to raise me the best way she knew how. As I got older, I grasped the realization to the statement I made pertaining to the way Mama raised me, "the best way she knew how." Later in life, I understood that Mama either raised me the way her mother raised her or tried to raise me better. Either way, I knew I could no longer hold Mama at fault for doing what she thought was best for me.

Before I move

forward, I want to tell someone reading this book that you cannot continue walking through life blaming your mother for the mistakes she made years ago. You cannot continue to blame her for your mistakes in life. You need to forgive her and move on. Let me be the first to tell you that your mother and your past is no longer holding you back from your future and your potential, but now it is your own unforgiveness and bitterness. You have to make the conscious decisions to forgive your mother and no one else can make that decision for you, but you. I guarantee you that if you forgive your mother, the heartaches that you been having for periods of years will stop. The blood clots will disappear. The cancer that your doctors are telling you that you have are connected to the unforgiveness that you have allowed to sit on your heart, and it is now eating at your heart, and bitterness has now sunk in your heart, but I promise you, if you make the conscious decision to forgive your mother, your health issues will disappear. Lastly, let me to tell you, your mother may never give you the apology that you have been waiting for years it may never come, but to free yourself from the hurt and bondage of the pain, you have to forgive her and let go.

****

It was hard for any person growing up in the projects to try to raise their children correctly, especially when their parents never raised them as such. We had a lot of this in the projects. Though things like this were always present, still it was never confronted. As I stated before, everybody in the projects were alcoholics, drug addicts, drug dealers or some of all three. This was normal to me and everybody else in the projects. When I would see dope fiends nodding in the streets, I didn't really comprehend what I was seeing until I got old enough to realize all that was taking place around me. Though I was a child, I was exposed to some things that I know for sure could have sent

MERCEDES JOHNSON

me into a crazy institution or should have led me to an addiction to some form of drugs.

Yes, Mama was sweet, yet she had a side that was not to be messed with. I witnessed many people call mama evil. Not only was I present when people called Mama evil but I also witnessed Mama wish death upon a man, and no later than a couple days after, that man was found dead. I knew Mama didn't mean it. I watched her silently that night drink herself into a deeper depression than she was already in. I remember hearing Mama repeatedly say, "I didn't mean it. He just made me so mad. I didn't mean it. I didn't mean it." She repeated these words over and over through sobs and slurs.

As I silently listened to Mama cry in the dark from my room, I remember feeling heaviness came upon my heart, and my heart began to ache. I wished that Mama didn't have to go through or experience the pain and regret that she was going through.

HERSTORY BREAKING THROUGH DARKNESS

I hated when Mama cried. I hated it. I wish I was able to do something to take the pain away. Once again, I knew that I couldn't.

I remember that night I laid by my door and listened to Mama's sniffles and whispers until I heard her finally get up from the table and staggered her way into her room. It didn't take Mama long to go to sleep. As soon as her body hit the bed, I heard her snoring. Once I heard Mama snoring, I then made my way to the bed, and I tried forcing myself to go to sleep, but I couldn't. It was hard to do so. Every time I closed my eyes, I kept seeing Mama sitting in a chair at the dining room table with her tall can of Olde English 800, with tears pouring down her face. Every time I saw Mama, I broke down crying. I remember an aching pain grasping my chest as if it was poking at my heart. The pain was violently extreme and brutal. I wanted to let out a loud cry, but I didn't want to awaken Mama. I placed one hand over my mouth and placed the other one on my chest

MERCEDES JOHNSON

while lying in pain, with tears flooding my face. I wanted the pain to go away more than anything. I didn't know where it came from, but I knew that it was real and the pain was excruciating.

I now understand that the pain I was feeling was the exact same pain Mama was experiencing. I never really understood why in the world at such a young age I carried all of Mama's burdens and weight. The sad thing about this was that I don't know if Mama knew that I was. One thing for sure is that I wasn't able to recognize this until years later. All the pain and hurt that I was witnessing Mama suffer was the same hurt and pain I began suffering on her behalf.

I want to tell someone that generational curses need to broken now in the name of Jesus. You cannot go a day longer carrying the same experiences and burdens and hurt that you mother, grandmother and great grandmother carried. I break that

HERSTORY BREAKING THROUGH DARKNESS

generational curse now in the mighty name of Jesus. You will not be a victim of your parents and grandparents mistakes, addictions and burdens. I declare your freedom in your mind, spirit, soul, wealth and health in the name of Jesus. Amen.

****

Once again, Mama was young when she had me; Daddy was even younger than Mama. The two of them was in their early teens, sixteen and seventeen.

When I turned four years old, Daddy was taken to prison and accused for attempt murder and sentenced to serve nine years in the penitentiary.

I don't know if the absence of Daddy ever affected me because all I knew was Mama. I hardly remembered anything about Daddy. Mama never really talked about him or had any pictures of him. Only time Mama would talk about Daddy was when she would compare me to him in a disgusting manner. She would say things like, "Ugh, you look just like your dad when you do that." I knew I looked just like my dad, but I hated it because I saw that it didn't please Mama, and I went out my way to try to please her in every way possible. That was my desire and mission as a child.

See, I knew I looked like my dad not just because Mama always told me, but when people who knew my dad saw me the first thing they would say, " Dang you look just like your Dad," "You know you are your daddy's twin. He couldn't deny you if he tried," or they would say, "Wow, you are a spitting image of your pa." When people would say that internally, I rejected it. I didn't want to look like him, and I wished that people didn't say that because I knew Mama didn't like it.

I don't remember the type of relationship Daddy and Mama had, but from how Mama talked about him, she displayed that it wasn't a good one.

Whenever Mama

mentioned my dad, she spoke with so much hatred and disgust toward him. The way Mama talked about him, one wouldn't have known that they were ever in a relationship.

It's funny how influence can mold a person's thoughts and perspective on people and as well as one's self. I learned at a young age that parents' opinions and behavior can become the opinions and thoughts of their children, and if a parent isn't careful, this type of influence can turn into control and manipulation, which eventually leads to witchcraft.

Listen, witchcraft doesn't start or end with spells and potions. No, that is a lie from the devil himself. The root of witchcraft is control and manipulation. Some people can be born into a family of witchcraft. How? Because their grand parents manipulated and controlled their mother or father, and when they had their children, they controlled them. They controlled and micromanaged their every move. They told them what degree they should get when they got into college. They told them what type of person they wanted them to date. For years, these victims agreed to everything that their parents wanted them to do because they sought out their approval and acceptance, and the minute they made a decision for themselves, it felt like all hell broke loose.

Some of you have been through this. You never understood why it seemed like you could never please your parents if you weren't doing what they wanted you to do. There were times when they would turn your younger and older siblings against you. They made up lies about you and had your siblings thinking terrible things about you to the point that they lost respect for you. This is manipulation, control and brainwash, which is witchcraft and this must be identified and broken.

If this form of witchcraft is not broken off one's life, it would carry on generation after generation and you, as the individual, will find

HERSTORY BREAKING THROUGH DARKNESS

yourself controlling and manipulative within every relationship you partake in. For some people, you might not be the controlling and manipulative one, but it is easy for you to become victim in an emotional, physical, financial and spiritual abusive relationship.

If you perhaps have noticed that you or someone you know have come from a family that was extremely controlling, before I move forward, another way you can tell is if your husband or wife's parents has to have a say so with every decision that you all make, that's controlling and it's witchcraft. Once again, the root of witchcraft is control and manipulation. After reading the examples above, if you or someone you know have grown up in this type of environment or family, it must be exposed and broken because it is generational, and until you make the conscious decision to break it, this spirit will attach itself to your children and your children's children.

Father, in the name of Jesus, I come against the

spirit of witchcraft right now in the mighty name of Jesus. I break the spirit of control, manipulation, mental abuse, rejection, intimidation, and mind games right now in the mighty name of Jesus. I apply the blood of Jesus over every person who is reading this who has come from a controlling family. Lord, I break that strong hold off their mind right now in the name of Jesus. I cover their mind in the blood of Jesus. I break the spirit of victimization in the name of Jesus. I sever the plans of this spirit now. I strip it of its power now in the name of Jesus. Every foothold it has had in the lives and minds of your children, I break its illegal and legal placement in their lives now in the mighty now of Jesus. I apply the blood. I loose the blood now. I take power, dominion and authority over every active witch in the minds of your children, and I expel its power, influence, affluence and position in their lives and minds right now in the mighty name of Jesus. I decree it and declare it so in the name of Jesus. Amen

HERSTORY BREAKING THROUGH DARKNESS

****

I never really had a relationship with Daddy well at least not to my knowledge. As I stated earlier, I don't really remember much about Daddy. But the more I heard Mama talk about him, which wasn't a lot, but it didn't take long for Mama outlook on Daddy becoming my outlook and opinions toward him.

Before I knew it, Mama hatred towards Daddy became my hatred. He never done anything to me, but the fact I only heard negative things about him, I too looked upon him as a no-good. I never wanted to hear anything about him. I developed such hatred toward him to the point that I didn't even want to hear his name mentioned in my presence. I hated him. I hated anything and everything that Daddy was and used to be a part of.

Before daddy went to the penitentiary, he was affiliated with a notorious gang known as the "Gangster Disciples" here in Chicago. The fact that Daddy was

MERCEDES JOHNSON

associated with the Gangster Disciples, I grew a hard, cold and hatred toward them. I confidently hated everything that reminded me of him. My hatred toward him was pure hatred, and it grew daily every time I thought about him or heard his name being mentioned by family members or his friends that roamed the streets.

The most interesting part about my growing hatred toward Daddy was that it wasn't a hatred that I myself had toward him. As far as I knew, I didn't even know him. I didn't have a thought or feeling about him before I adapted Mama's attitude and feelings toward him. It was no different from any other situation like when Mama pain, hurt or feelings became mine. I don't believe Mama intentions was for me to hate Daddy as much as she did, but it wasn't long until I developed a pure hatred towards him. My hatred solidly sat upon my dark and cold heart.

I don't know if Mama noticed or sensed my hatred, but I remember one day it seemed as if she was testing my heart to see if my hatred for him was real.

There was a particular day when Mama and I were lounging around in the house, and she began to test me. I remember Mama and I didn't leave the house the whole day. As stated before, whenever Mama and I would stay in the house intentionally, we will lie around all day watching movies until the wee hours of the night.

As the sky began to darken, Mama and I slowly began to prepare to snuggle underneath each other. Oh how I loved lying under Mama in our huge comforters. I loved days like these. But this day was different from any other we spent together. This day in particular scarred my heart. Not only did it scar my heart, but it also birthed a certain type of feeling toward Mama that I wasn't able to comprehend until I got old enough to understand the taunting and hidden feelings I harbored in my heart toward her.

MERCEDES JOHNSON

"Jada," Mama called out to me in a jokingly voice.

"Yes ma'am," I replied to Mama as I walked into the room where she was lying in bed.

"Come here."

As I climbed in the bed with Mama, she quickly and playfully began attacking me. I remember yelling, screaming and laughing all at the same time. I loved when Mama gave me her undivided attention. Times like this wasn't an everyday or every week thing for Mama and I so I cherished them wholeheartedly. I loved Mama more than anything.

"Stop, stop, stop!" I yelled out through a mouthful of laughter. I was very ticklish in certain areas and Mama knew the exact places. She tickled me until my face became beet red and to the point I knew I was going to urine on myself.

"Stop, stop. I got to pee. I got to pee," I barely got my words out.

HERSTORY BREAKING THROUGH DARKNESS

Mama eventually stopped. The minute she stopped, I dashed out the bed and ran to the restroom. It was that serious.

When I came back to the room, Mama was sitting up looking in my direction. As I reentered into the room, I remember a smirk appeared on Mama's face.

"Do you love me?" Mama asked me with her eyes piercing through me.

"Yes ma'am. I love you so much, Mom," I said smiling from ear to ear. I was confident in the love I had for Mama.

"No, you don't," Mama replied.

I would have taken one of Mama's beatings that day because the pain that ripped through me was unidentifiable. The beatings from Mama were always identifiable and sometimes the pain felt as if they were unbearable. But this pain and this hurt was different. I couldn't understand why Mama would say that I didn't love her. Her words and rejection of my love pierced me right in my heart. It felt like a dagger was thrown at me and caught me directly in the heart. It felt like I was in the middle of a game of darts, and Mama's words were the darts and my heart was the target.

I ran to the bed where Mama was sitting with her same smirk across her face looking directly at me. As she stared at me, tears began to flood down my face, "Mom, I do love you. I do love you. I love you so much. I love you so much, Mom. I only love you," I repeatedly told her through my tears.

As I continued telling her I loved her, she shook her head no without hesitating. I remember my tears nearly choking me. It got to the point when I couldn't say anything because my tears were straining me. But whenever my airways were clear enough for me to prove my love to Mama, I did. My voice went from whining to yelling. I went from grabbing her hands to pulling on her hands. She needed to know that I loved her. I knew I did, but I wasn't convinced. Though I could've argued against my brutal and crucifying thoughts about Mama. Her facial expression never changed. If there happened to have been anything about Mama's facial expression, it was that her smirk got wider. Though I was only six or seven, I wasn't easily fooled and from the look in Mama's eyes; she was secretly enjoying torturing me.

No matter how loud I yelled out, "Mom, I love you." She continued to shake her head no. Even though she stared into my eyes and saw my hurt and my tears building and falling from the wells of my eyes, her expression never changed. Her smirk never left and the look in her eyes grew more intense.

"How much do you love me?" was the next question Mama asked while still piercing through me with her eyes. But this time, the smirk was gone and replaced with a stern look.

I couldn't believe what I was hearing. I couldn't believe Mama was really asking me this. All I knew was Mama. I never wanted to leave her sight. Darn it. I was her first and only child, and for sure, I didn't have another mother before her. All I knew was Mama!

"Mom," I whined as I climbed into the bed with her. I tried grabbing her into my small frail shaking arms, but in one swift move, she pulled away from me. This time, it felt like I was a faucet and someone left the water running. My tears poured out of me uncontrollably. I was hurt. My very soul was hurt. I couldn't muster up the words to express how I was feeling. It was a feeling that I dare not wish upon any other person.

As Mama and I stared into one another's eyes, her smirk appeared again. I'm not sure which one I despised more- her smirk or the stern look- and neither of the looks did not display Mama's love that I knew she had for me.

"You don't love me. You love your dad more than me." From the look in Mama's eyes and on her face, I would have sworn that this amused her.

"Mom… No, I don't. I don't love him more than you. Mom, I don't love him. I only love you, Mom. I don't love him." I was in my convincing state once again.

Mama sat up in the bed laughing as she watched me, rant over and over how I didn't love my dad and how I loved her more.

"No you don't," Mama responded to my ranting while slowly shaking her head left to right.

I didn't understand. I barely knew my dad. I saw pictures of him and visited him in prison two or three times when his mother, my grandmother went to visit him. Even then, I still didn't build a relationship with him during the few times of seeing him. Our visits did not leave any type of impact on me or opened an interest within me to want to get to know him more. My developed hatred towards him had already taken its course- full course to be exact.

While laughing Mama said, "if you love me, you will go get me a glass of cold ice water."

That was my cue right there. I tried to get out the bed too fast and found myself on the floor. I crawled on my knees out of the room. Once I got outside the room, I jumped on my feet and sprinted to the kitchen and made Mama ice-cold water and returned to her in a nick of time.

When I made it back to the room, Mama smirk was plastered on her face again.

"Here, Mom," I said almost in a whisper.

She couldn't hold it in anymore. Before I knew it, Mama was full of laughter. She was doubled over, holding her stomach laughing. I looked at her with a confused look on my face. I began to look around the room. I was trying to figure out what was it that I missed. After Mama got done laughing, she stretched her arms out toward me, motioning me to come to her.

"Yes, ma'am," I said while slowly walking toward her. I don't know why, but I was scared. I didn't know what to think. Mama was acting different than any other day. I couldn't put my finger on it, but I know it made me feel uncomfortable.

"Come here, girl," Mama spoke out with a loud voice as if she was irritated.

I moved faster when I heard the sound of her voice. When I got closer to her, she grabbed me and wrapped me in her arms tightly.

"I love you too, baby," she said, while holding me in her arms.

I thought I was done crying until then. My hot tears filled the wells of my eyes and fell down my face continuously. I wrapped my arms around Mama's neck and held unto her as if it was going to be the last time I would

MERCEDES JOHNSON

ever hug her. As I hugged her, I didn't realize how relieved and at ease I felt in that instance. It felt so good to feel loved and embraced by Mama again. Never again did I want to play Mama's amusement game anymore. I liked it more like this.

For the remaining of the night, Mama and I stayed up watching movies until we fell asleep. This night Mama fell asleep first while I stayed up. I couldn't help but to think about what took place this evening between Mama and I. At first, I tried to brush the scenes and thoughts out my mind, but as I laid on my back looking toward the ceiling, the words, "you don't love me," kept finding their way to my frontal lobe. I figured something must have been wrong with me so I tried lying on my side looking toward Mama. As soon as I looked in Mama's direction, tears immediately began to fall. I couldn't shake the ache of pain I felt as I looked at her.

I couldn't

HERSTORY BREAKING THROUGH DARKNESS

understand. I couldn't understand why Mama behaved the way she did toward me. I wonder did she understand how she made me feel or did that really amuse her.

The longer I looked at Mama; my mind raced with questions that I knew was never going to get answered. Mama really didn't love me. If she did, she wouldn't have hurt me the way she did. Love don't hurt, at least it wasn't supposed to hurt. Love doesn't reject you and make you cry. All these things that love didn't do, Mama was doing them.

I battled with these thoughts not just for this night but also for the remaining of my days. The words she spoke, the rejection she displayed wounded me in a way that I wasn't able to identify at the time. Mama's rejection seeped into my heart and conscious. Her rejection wrapped and molded itself within me and around me.

As you can see, it wasn't just hurt and pain that became a part of my life by the time I was five and up, but

MERCEDES JOHNSON

this day, I met rejection face- to- face. It wasn't a pretty sight. Rejection wasn't anywhere near friendly nor did it pretend to be friendly. Rejection hated me and wanted me dead. He wanted me to himself. Rejection was more selfish than hurt and pain. Rejection was selfish and stubborn. He didn't care about no one but himself. He was self-gratifying and wanted all the attention on himself. Whenever someone else got more attention than him, he downplayed the person so that the individual could feel bad about himself or herself. Eventually, the individual would not want to get attention anymore because to them it was associated with rejection, self-rejection.

Rejection was cruel, and he didn't play fair. He made you feel like everybody hated you and that no one cared about you. He used this method or strategy to get you to the point of isolating yourself from everyone that tries to get close to you.

This is rejection. He

HERSTORY BREAKING THROUGH DARKNESS

invaded my life at the age six or seven. This night, when Mama rejected me was the beginning of when rejection introduced himself and became a part of my life, mind, heart and relationships. Rejection became a part of me.

Many of you may be thinking how did I know this at such a young age. Well, I will tell you. The day Mama rejected me opened the door for rejection himself to invade my life. He didn't just invade my life, but he made sure his thoughts, opinions and voice was heard out loud and clear.

I remember that night I wrestled with crazy thoughts of self-condemnation. I made up my mind that something must have been wrong with me if Mama didn't love me. I realized that I wasn't good enough to be loved if Mama didn't want to love me. I didn't deserve to be loved.

As I battled with these inner and mental battles, it didn't take long before I began I accepted them as truth, and I slowly began to reject and hate myself.

Though Mama might have been playing or

whatever the case might have been, but for me that night changed the way I looked at myself. It took something from me. From that night forward I lived my life trying to prove myself to others. I never thought I was good enough for people. I always thought of excuses why people didn't or wouldn't like me. There were times when I would reject myself before I gave others the chance to get to know me.

As you can see, rejection took over my whole being. It took over my thoughts toward myself as well others. This spirit contaminated my relationship with others. I didn't know how to be friend people. I pushed people away before a friendship could even develop. My trust as a child was damaged and completely destroyed. It was hard for me to trust because the trust that I had with Mama no longer existed. It had vanished. I couldn't tell you when my trust toward Mama left, but I do know that at the time, it wasn't of my own choice. My trust along with half of my identity was snatched from me without my consent. I don't know if Mama noticed when my behavior and attitude had shifted, and if she didn't notice, I know I surely did.

MERCEDES JOHNSON

3
The Deeper The Seed The Deeper The Dig
~ ~ ~ ~

BEFORE WE DIG deeper, let me remind you, these events I tell you about took place when I was between the ages four to eight. See, I didn't grow up with a silver spoon in my mouth. I didn't grow up with Mommy and Daddy in the house. I didn't grow up with a hot meal cooked everyday when I got home everyday. No! I was lucky enough Mama was at the house when I got out of school. That type of life didn't exist for me. I didn't know anything about marriage, careers, or college. Success didn't exist. That type of talk didn't exist where I was from. All I knew was dope fiends, crackheads, drug dealers, GDs (Gangster

HERSTORY BREAKING THROUGH DARKNESS

Disciples), BDs (Black Disciples), the police, shootouts, drunks, molesters, fights, and everything else one can imagine or maybe not imagine.

 This was my surroundings. Robert Taylor Projects wasn't a place for anyone to have grown up in especially a child. Before I made it to middle school, I saw my first dead body. The crime scenes in the projects were real. It wasn't a joke. The crazy thing about all this is how people became immune to it. This type of living was normal. This is what happened to me.

 This type of lifestyle was normal to me, and I loved it. At the time, I wouldn't have changed it for nothing in the world. Myself, along with the other kids my age thought it was funny and exciting when the different project buildings and the police would have shootouts. These shootouts went on for days. Sometimes, we couldn't go to school because the wars would be so bad. As crazy as it may sound, I loved it when it was wartime. It brought out an excitement from

MERCEDES JOHNSON

the inside of me as well as other young people my age.

If you don't mind, allow me to enhance your horizon and bring you to one of the nights during the shootouts.

Every streetlight on the corners was gone out, meaning it was dark outside and typically during these times and days, you will not find anyone outside in sight. Everybody in the projects knew what time it was. The Black Disciples and the police had been in war for close to a week.

I remember this night like it was yesterday. Myself and some other kids were on the elevator going up to the thirteenth floor. While on the elevator, it stopped and the doors opened up and one of the BDs ran on the elevator with a gun that stood from the ground to his waist.

"What's up, Mane," I said, eyeing his gun with my eyes wide open like a kid inside a candy store.

"What's up, Jada," he responded with a smile.

HERSTORY BREAKING THROUGH DARKNESS

See Mane was older than me, but he wasn't past twenty-one. Some people would consider him still a baby. In reality, Mane wasn't by far the youngest in the buildings that ran with the BDs. There were other boys in the buildings who were younger and were sometimes forced to become a BD whether they wanted to or not.

Mane didn't stay on the elevator with us long. He got off the very next stop. As soon as he got off the other kids and I who were on the elevator hysterically blurted out talking about how big Mane's gun was. We talked about it until we made it to our destination. His gun was a sight to see for us.

Once we made it on the thirteenth floor, the excitement started for us. Other kids were already on the porch with their hands holding on to the steel-looking fence. The war was taking place right in front of us. Bullets were flying left to right. We saw some of the gang members we knew crouching down behind objects so that

MERCEDES JOHNSON

the police wouldn't see them. They were trying to get good aims.

I remember standing on the porch with other kids jumping up and down whenever we saw a police get shot. To us, the police was the enemies. Whenever you saw a cop in the projects, it meant bad business, and everybody knew not to talk to the cops ever. The projects was so secure that whenever a police car would drive past on the file line or in front of the projects, there was a special code that would be shouted. This code would be shouted to the people who were serving dope fiends at the time. Everybody knew the code - even us - and we weren't even dealers or bangers, but I guess in heart we were.

Nights like these, we listened to the bullets blasting, and they sounded like music to our ears. Many of us didn't know what was really going on, but one thing for sure, it was something that we got use to and we became immune to it. Though people were dying left and right, the drug game was real. The addiction to dope and the money was real. No matter how many friends or family members were lost during the wars and no matter how many dead bodies baby mamas cried over and fought over, business were still in operation. Dope fiends were everywhere. If I'm not mistaken, there were probably more dope fiends than alcoholics, and trust and believe me, there were a lot of them.

See, in the Robert Taylor Projects, each building had sixteen floors, and I guarantee on every floor, there was at least one boarded-up apartment. I never understood why they would board them up when majority of them will be turned into dope houses or apartments where the young BDs would hang in. They called it the spot.

I remember the night during the war between the BDs and the police; it went on all night until the morning. I swear you would have sworn that their battles were strategic because the war and shootouts only took place at night when the streetlights went out. If you weren't back at the buildings before the streetlights went out, your best bet was to stay where you were. No one dared to get caught between the crossfire.

The next morning, my cousins and I got dressed and ready for school. We went to a public school where all the BD building and some GD building kids went to. Trust me, there were fights during school, before school, and after school everyday. There wasn't a day that went by that there wasn't a fight. It wasn't just boys fighting, but girls too. Matter of fact, it was more girl fights than boys. The school we went to, I guess, didn't believe in suspending kids because sometimes it would be the same girls and boys fighting back to back. The funny thing about this was that majority of the times the people who were fighting was family.

However, on this particular morning, I believe we were running late for breakfast at school, I remember making it down to the first floor before my cousins. As I made it to the first floor, a lot of people were crowded around screaming, hollering and crying out, "No." I remember hearing the sirens from the paramedics outside of the building. As I made my way through the crowd, I found myself face-to-face with a young man I knew who was a friend of the family. He was tied to a chair with duct tape wrapped around him with a bullet in his head-center forehead to be exact.

As I looked at him, I stood frozen for what felt like minutes, and I remember having no feelings, no sorrow and no remorse it was as if I was numb. For me to have been so young, I was use to this, and I knew the rules of the gang and the streets all too well. I understood as bad or mean this might sound, but I knew he was just another person that died to the streets. Though many people yelled and cried, it didn't take long for everybody to pretend that he had never died. Death was something that no one seemed to have feared in the projects. Death was always lurking around the buildings, and it was up to you not to get caught.

When I you tell you that death was everywhere, I tell you no lie. It felt like everybody lived his or her life trying to stay on top of the drug gang and run away from death. What everybody failed to realize was that death was right at his or her front door, waiting for the right time to come in. See, death played his cards strategically in the projects. While everyone thought they were out running death, they were befriending him. Everyone was too blinded to see that death wasn't just a part of the shootouts, the wars between the BDs and GDs, or the gangs and the police, but it was deeper than that. Death had a hold and a control system within the buildings, community and people within the projects. Everybody there was under the control and choke hold of death. One of his slow death holds that he had on everyone was the lost of hope.

It was very rare to

find anyone who had hope to want more or better yet, even see on achieving in life. The projects were like a cemetery, and everyone was like zombies. They were dead men walking.

As children, we didn't have role models, positive influences, or leaders growing up. The projects were a system that was sat up for our demise. It was sat up for death and destruction as its pillars, and we fail right in their traps. No one had jobs, and if they did, it was probably 15 percent out of 100 percent who had jobs. Everyone was on welfare, receiving government assistance like WIC, real food stamps in paper form and cash on the link card. Government assistance was considered a check to those who got it. The sad thing about this was the fact that they only received it once a month. It was really sad for those who were strung out on dope and had kids because it was rare that their kids saw food or their parents around the time the checks came. The parents would wait for the

MERCEDES JOHNSON

mailman, go to curse exchange, cash their check, sometimes sell their food stamps and spend all their money on dope, alcohol, and get high and drunk for days until all their check was gone.

These were the type of parents most of us were dealing with in the projects. I will not say that every parent did dope, and if they didn't, they were alcoholics. I couldn't even tell you which one was worst. I knew I hated both of them, and I knew that both of these weapons were the weapons that death was using as a slow death, which everybody failed to realize. Though they weren't dying a fast death like those in the wars, they were living a slow death daily. If I had a choice, I probably would have chosen a fast instant death with a stray bullet, but you see, that was the problem here. None of us had a choice in the matter, especially us children. We were born into this death system, and we had to learn the rules of survival fast. The sad thing about this was the fact that everybody knew each other. Everyone knew everyone, yet at the same time it was a dog-eat-dog world, every man for himself or herself. Though it was sad, it was the truth. You had to learn the rules of the streets, and you had to learn fast. The funny thing about this code and mentality was that you didn't have to worry about those who didn't know you, but you had to watch those who smiled and laughed with you. You had to watch those who grew up with you. These were the same people who scrapped food from the bottom of the barrel with you. In the projects, the proverb was true when people say, "You have to keep your friends close and your enemies closer." You may have grown up with someone, but at the end of the day those who you thought were for you were the ones who were really against you and waiting in the garden like a snake to see you fall.

    I had to learn quickly. If the projects never taught me anything, one thing it did teach me was not to fear death. I know some of you may be thinking like I'm crazy or over exaggerated, but I'm not. See, death is more than just seeing a physical body in the grave or casket. I understood death on many and multiple dimensions. I also understood that death didn't only come to kill you with a stray bullet or a sharp knife, but it also came to kill you slowly. I understood that death wasn't always dark, with dark shades and a hoodie to cover his face, but sometimes death came in a disguise a bright light, huge smile and a wicked plan to destroy your life. I understood that death would come to befriend you when you were at your weakest and feed you lies so that you can begin to deceive yourself and believe his lies.

    I understood death to be a deceiver, a liar, a back bitter, a manipulator and most of all, a snake that could transform itself as a sheep, a friend and whatever else you may need in your life at the time. Death's appearance wasn't and isn't always as ugly as people think. Though his motives were pure evil, he appeared to bring peace.

Death was risen, alive and thriving throughout the projects. He became friends with everybody here. There wasn't a person whom he

didn't manipulate and control. He used the drug dealers and gang bangers as his puppets. He fed them lies and had them thinking that the life they was living was going to deliver them from poverty. So they sold dope and heroin to every addict that came their way including their own family members. Death was using them to feed these people who felt trapped in the system of poverty, depression and oppression, and before they knew it, they were trapped in an addiction that was sat up by death himself. He was setting up traps to kill them slowly.

It didn't take long when death eventually invited his fellow workers: hatred, bitterness, and resentment into his plot. When hatred joined the team, he entered in full force.

MERCEDES JOHNSON

Hatred alone hovered over every heart who dwelt in the projects. It was easy for hatred to find his place in every young and old person's heart due to the system of poverty within the projects. The adult parents had given up on hope and turned to drugs and alcohol. The adult priorities weren't the well-being of their children; it was when and how they were going to get their next hit or drink. This was painful as a child to watch your mother, father or family member in general, to throw their life away in this type of manner. It wasn't long until the kids eventually learn quickly that they had to make a living for him or herself. We had to take care of ourselves because Mama or Daddy wasn't there to be the parents that we needed them to be. This hurt.

Listen, no child was ever made or fit for this type of responsibility. This is when hatred began to enter in and manipulate the mind and heart of the children in the projects, including myself.

HERSTORY BREAKING THROUGH DARKNESS

As you can see, it wasn't hard for hatred to rule and reign over us in the projects. It wasn't hard at all. And if someone were to ask us questions regarding our hatred, we all felt as if we had every right to be full of anger, hate, hurt, resentment, bitterness and murder. It was easy to put the blame on our parents, and of course, our parents blamed their parents. Can you see the generational curse? Can you see the unforgiveness, which was one of the underlying working of a lot of the flared emotions that came forth from the kids and our parents?

Though we might have thought we had every right to these feelings, they did not serve anyone justice. It wasn't long until we took our hurt and frustration out on everyone around us including ourselves. See, when hatred entered in, he birthed within us division, but not your ordinary division between gang member or gang members and police. But what he brought was division amongst family members- mothers versus daughters, fathers versus

MERCEDES JOHNSON

sons, and cousins versus cousins. The war within our hearts was real due to the hurt and pain, which created the path for many of us to walk in pure hatred.

Since death was leading us, he was also planting seeds of evil and murder in our minds. Once again, let's get this understood, death was clever. He didn't say, "I feel like outing dude right there on the spot." No! He was too clever for that. See, he would rather watch us torment one another by selling dope to each other's family. Or we as children had to watch our parents spend all the money on liquor and drugs, or he will send a rapist in the building to run around at night, raping little girls and boys. These were some of the things he loved and enjoyed watching. These were the seeds he plotted and as the seeds were being sown, they birthed out a full manifestation of hatred and a hardness of heart that was secured by bitterness and resentment. Before we were given the chance to realize what was going on, we no longer wasn't just caged

HERSTORY BREAKING THROUGH DARKNESS

within the walls of a ghetto, but we became incarcerated by our own thoughts and motives.

Our thoughts stemmed from the hurt and pain, which caused us to build up walls of unforgiveness and trust issues. We built our own prisons in our own hearts.

MERCEDES JOHNSON

4
The System of Bondage
~ ~ ~ ~

SEE, WHAT MANY failed to realize is the fact that, over the years, a ghetto is far more than just a gated community or building. It is so much more than just one's environment. It actually becomes a part of your mentality. It seeps into your life, your personality, your relationships and your self-esteem. Spiritually, the word *ghetto* is tied into the family and system of bondage.

Allow me to open your horizon to the spirit realm of the manifestation of ghetto and projects. When you are dealing with ghettos and projects, you are dealing with a spirit of bondage, poverty, control, manipulation and death. However, the more interesting truth of this revelation is that these spirits are abiding under a demonic governmental system.

In order for a governmental system to operate, there have to be a hierarchy controlling the system. So we know that there have to be a hierarchy. Okay. So as mentioned earlier, this system and government

is demonic, meaning before everything was manifested here on the earth it was already formulated in the spirit realm (in the heavens).

In the book of Ephesians chapter 6, the order of Satan is laid out for us to see. "For we wrestle not against flesh and blood, but against principalities, against powers, against the rulers of the darkness of this world, against spiritual wickedness in high places" (Eph. 6:12). This scripture highlights to us the order, the strategic movement how Satan government system is sat up in the heavens.

Within each demonic system, it is strategically sat up how Ephesians 6:12 explains to us. Before I move further, I will like to point out that principalities are governmental/ territorial spirits that hover over regions, states, cities, nations, etc.

In the book of Daniel chapter 10, it says,

Then he continued, "Do not be afraid, Daniel. Since the first day that you set your mind to gain understanding and to humble yourself before God, your words were heard, and I have come in response to them. But the prince of the Persian kingdom resisted me twenty-one days. Then Michael, one of the Chief Princes, came to help me, because I was detained there with the King of Persia,"(Dan. 10:12-13, NIV).

When the angel Gabriel (the messenger) came to Daniel, he explained to him, the reason it took him so long to respond to his prayer was because the prince of Persian kingdom was blocking him for twenty-one days. In this context, the prince of Persia was not flesh and blood, but it was a principality, a governmental and territorial spirit that was standing and blocking the airwaves. His job was to block any and every message of hope to the people and Daniel. The Prince of the Persian Kingdom countered anything that was of God. Before anything is manifested in the physical, it has already happened in the heavens (the realm of the Spirit).

I know you may be wondering what does all this has to do with anything. Well, it has a lot to do with everything that I have explained from the beginning to now.

Okay, so let's draw our mind and eyes back on the Robert Taylor projects for a minute. As stated earlier, the foundation of the projects was death itself. Once again, when I say death, it doesn't technically mean physical death, but spiritual death. It was spiritual death because there was such a separation and disconnection from God. Growing up, I didn't hear about God (Jesus) until I got older, and even then, I thought Jesus was a myth that African Americans made up. I was clueless about Jesus as well as the devil. I didn't know that any of that existed. All I knew was to live for today and worry about tomorrow when it come. That was my motivation growing up in the projects.

The fact that it was such a spiritual death, it was as if everyone was walking zombies. If the spirit of God is life (which He is) and everyone was without the spirit of God (life), that meant we were walking around already dead. So if we're walking around without the spirit of God and we're spiritually dead, physically, we were dying slowly. We didn't have anything to look forward to, and the fact that there was nothing that was pressing or pushing us to want to go forward, it didn't matter if we lived to see the next day or not.

HERSTORY BREAKING THROUGH DARKNESS

It's important to understand that when there's a separation between mankind and God, destruction will be the guidance. The mind will be hovered over by death.

We now have an understanding that the foundation in the projects were death. Now allow me to take you a little deeper. Though the foundation was death, death was not the governmental spirit that hovered over the projects. Many of you might be surprised when I reveal unto you the spirit that hovered over the Robert Taylor Projects. I must admit, I myself was a bit surprised when the Lord revealed unto me the domineering spirit. This territorial and governmental spirit is no other than the spirit of poverty.

MERCEDES JOHNSON

5
Invasion of Poverty
~ ~ ~ ~

POVERTY'S JOB IS to strip an individual, city, region and country of their sense of direction. It places blinders on one's eyes and cause one to stumble into financial and mental pits. Once one falls into a financial pit, it binds that individual mentality and injects itself within that person.

I know this may sound foreign to some of you, and you are ready to put this book down. But I urge you not to do so and continue reading. This is going to help some of you. Trust me.

Now, when the spirit of poverty injects itself within

an individual, a soul tie in the spirit realm is then formed. The interesting thing about this type of soul tie- the Lord revealed unto me- is that once poverty get's a hold of someone, it clings unto that person and releases itself into the bloodstream of the individual. Once that is done, it not only creates a soul tie, but a blood covenant is in agreement that eventually turn into a generational curse.

Too many people have believed the lie and hype of generational curses not being real, but turn around and have the audacity to speak out their mouth generational blessings. How in the word do you believe in one and not the other? Listen, let me explain something to some of you. We serve an all-knowing and powerful God, meaning whenever God set order in the earth realm, there too was disorder in the world. When God created good, evil was present as well. When He created righteousness, unrighteousness was created as well. Many of you are looking confused to this concept and that is okay. A lot of

MERCEDES JOHNSON

us have been told about free will and how God has given us free will correct? I want you to ask yourself if God only created light without darkness, righteousness without unrighteousness and so on, don't you think that would defeat the purpose and principle of free will if God wouldn't have placed in front of us options to choose from?

What does all this mean? It simply means that there are generational blessings as well as generational curses.

The spirit of poverty is also a spirit of bondage. It is a mental bondage more than anything. Not only does this spirit enslave its victims, but it also robs one of their success, confidence, integrity and most of all, their self-esteem. It drains the strength and motivation out of one's body. Poverty lingers and tries to leech unto whoever is connected to its victims. He's a generational spirit. Once poverty traps his victims, his goal is to bind up the whole family including close friends.

Just like death was

HERSTORY BREAKING THROUGH DARKNESS

real and alive in the projects, poverty was as well. See, when poverty blinded our eyes in the projects and began to guide us, our parents felt like there was only one way to escape the reality of this bondage. Their escape route was to turn to drugs and alcohol. While our parents turned to those things, we turned to the streets and became closer to hatred and death. These two were no longer just acquaintances, but they had become our close friends and leaders.

For anyone who have lived in these projects and survived, I truly give honor to them with all respect. How many of you have heard of the proverb, "You can take the person out the ghetto, but you can't take the ghetto out the person?" As cliché as that might sound, let me be the first to say I agree with that totally.

As I stated in the previous pages, poverty is a generational spirit that lingers. One can still be under subjection to this spirit if they move physically from the projects and move to the best state there is. Poverty is going to still be there. It doesn't matter if one gets a good paying job; poverty will always tell you that the payment is still not enough. No matter how much money one makes, that individual will never think it's enough. Another thing is that when one has money in their possession, they will spend it as soon as they get it. They start back at zero. These are some examples when an individual is still stuck in a financial pit and is bind by poverty.

Poverty is a mentality. It starts with how one think. If one plans to break free from the spirit of poverty, you have to start with your thinking pattern. The mind must be transformed. "And be ye not conformed to this world: but be ye transformed by the renewing of your mind, that ye prove what is that good, and acceptable, and perfect, will of God," (Rom. 12:2). The Bible also reminds us in the book of 2 Corinthians 10,

For the weapons of

our warfare are not carnal, but mighty through God to the pulling down of strong holds; Casting down imaginations, and every high thing that exalteth itself against the knowledge of God, and bringing into captivity every thought to the obedience of Christ. (2 Cor. 10:4-5)

Listen, poverty is a spirit, meaning you cannot get rid of poverty by gaining a certain of money; we cannot fight this spirit with carnal/material things. Since this spirit lies dormant in our minds, we have to transform our minds, according to Romans 12:2, with the word of God as well as pull down that strong hold once again with the word of God.

One cannot run from this spirit. One cannot try to buy this spirit out of their life. Why? Because it is a generational spirit, and generational spirits grow and forms into a generational curse. On a deeper scale, spiritually somewhere down the line in one's family lineage, a blood

MERCEDES JOHNSON

covenant was created, which makes this spirit feel entitled to one's life and family.

As you all can see, the projects was more than just a building. Though many people have their ideas of how it might have been living in the projects, let me tell you all something you'll never truly understand how it was. You'll never understand how it felt to live in such a demonic system that was formed from the beginning for your failure, destruction and death. The funny thing about all of this is that once one is trapped within these buildings- these demonic encroachments and lifestyle- a person never sees beyond these four walls. One never realizes that there's something greater than what has been presented. Once one realizes that there are greater things in life outside of these four walls, all the confidence that they once had has already been destroyed. So even when one realize that there is greatness inside of them, they find it hard to believe that they deserve better.

HERSTORY BREAKING THROUGH DARKNESS

Like I said in the beginning, when introducing poverty more than anything, poverty attack one's mind. In the mind. It creates invisible barriers and strongholds. Strongholds are lies that have been spoken over someone for so long that the individual starts to believe the lie. Once the individual embrace the lie as truth, that's when the stronghold is built into barriers or a fortress. See, in the beginning when the lies are first being spoken over an individual life, strongholds are not built, but seeds are planted. It is only when the person embraces or accepts the lies as truth that is when the strongholds begin to form. When the stronghold forms, there's a spirit that enters in and hovers over the person's mind in that particular compartment of the mind. For example, if all your life you have been told that you will never be anything. The more you hear it, you eventually begin to believe it. Once you believe it, that indicates that you have embraced it as your personal truth. The fact that it is truth to you, it hovers over your system of thinking and blind your eyes. Once your eyes are blinded with lies, it makes it impossible for you to see beyond the lies. When this happens, it is obvious that a stronghold has been sat in place. It is obvious because it is the stronghold that creates the blinders over your eyes.

In literal terms, the individual mind is hovered with lies about themselves or even about others that they have accepted as truth. The only way that these strongholds can be brought down is the Word of God, which is truth. This is the only escape way out because the strongholds and lies bring about a dark presence over the person's mind, meaning there's a dark force that resides within the individual. It can only take light and truth to expose darkness and lies. Once you begin to release the Word of God against the lies that have clouded your mind, the strongholds then begin to lose its grip, and the lies starts to be trampled down by the Word of God, which is truth. Once this begin to happen,

HERSTORY BREAKING THROUGH DARKNESS

the overpowering dark force that resided in you begins to get shaky, and it can no longer stand as firm as before because now the power of God is overpowering the force that once was overpowering you. The truth shall make you free.

It is imperative that I broke this down before moving to the next part of the book. Before I move on, I just want to tell someone who is reading this book that you're not what people have said that you are. You are not what they have labeled you as a child. I decree and declare that you are more than a conqueror. I speak to every stronghold in your life and mind right now that you will not be bound to their lies or influences any longer. I decree and declare that this is your day of freedom. I don't care if you have dealt with this thing for all of your life, with the power and authority invested in me, I speak to every obstacle and situation in your life and declare that you are free right now in the name of Jesus. I release the blood of

Jesus over you right now. I decree and declare that the fire of the Holy Ghost now diminish every tormenting thought. Every thought of suicide is ceased right now in the mighty name of Jesus. I speak to you right now and declare that you arise from this place of misery and pity. So what if people hate on you. So what if people reject you. So what if people don't want to be around you. So what. I hear the Lord say, "It's time to get up and take up your bed. It's time to get up and take up your bed and don't look back. I charge your spirit today that you take up your bed and never look back at yesterday because yesterday is gone and your sins have been forgiven and your strongholds have been diminished." This day, our Father has placed a new day and life ahead of you. I charge your spirit to grasp the hand of God right now and allow Him to lead and guide you to your next divine appointment with Him. Destiny is calling you. In Jesus name, Amen.

HERSTORY BREAKING THROUGH DARKNESS

EVERYTHING ISN'T AS PRETTY AS THE OUTSIDE

MERCEDES JOHNSON

1
The Sugar Isn't Always Sweet
~ ~ ~ ~

Ain't no sunshine when she's gone

She's always gone too long anytime she goes away

BILL WITHERS COULDN'T have written this song any better than how he wrote it. The words of this song drew and described the feeling I secretly felt toward Mama. I couldn't articulate if I should have given up on us spending time together or not because from the looks how things were going this issue was going, this issue was going to continue to be the battle for the two of us or maybe just me. I couldn't understand why Mama continued drinking no matter how many times I came to her begging and crying for her to stop. I couldn't grasp the idea that the only relationship Mama and I was going to have was me watching her drink her life away from a distance.

Please don't get me wrong. I loved mama with all of my heart. The quality times and moments that we did share together was amazing. I didn't take these moments and times for granted, but what I am saying is that Mama wasn't ready to be a mother, and I had to deal with these consequences. I am not playing the blame game, but I am identifying the pains I had to endure because of the pain and struggles my mother had to endure. I wasn't exempt by a long shot.

There was one particular time when Mama and I sat

MERCEDES JOHNSON

down, and I expressed to her how I wanted her to stop drinking, and to my surprise Mama promised me that she would try to stop. Mama took her promise to me serious and the both of us started attending a church on the Southside of Chicago. This lasted for about two to three weeks. During this time, Mama kept her words and did not touch a bottle of liquor or a can of beer. I was so happy for her. We spent more time together during those times as well. I don't remember what it was that ticked Mama off, but I know this didn't last long.

During this stage and time of Mama's life I remember seeing her on the floor in her room crying. When I walked into her bedroom she was balled up in a fetus position. I watched her in silence. I stood and watched Mama cry out in pain and agony. I don't know how I knew it, but I knew that Mama was fighting the urge not to drink. I remember standing there with tears running down my face. I wanted to take the

HERSTORY BREAKING THROUGH DARKNESS

pain away from her. For the first time in my life at that moment, I wanted to give Mama a drink to take her pain away. I wanted it all to go away. I wanted Mama to be strong enough to fight the addiction, but at that very moment, I understood that she couldn't do it on her own.

I know that I am not the only one who have a parent who was or is still addicting to alcohol or drugs, and to us who aren't addicted, we think that it should be easy for them to just stop, but it isn't that easy. There is someone who is still angry with his or her mother because your mother never showed you or your other siblings the attention that you all needed, and she spent all her money on liquor. There has even been times when you all went days without food, and you had to find ways for you all to eat. Over time, your misunderstanding and hurt grew into anger, pain, unforgiveness and hatred toward your mother. Over time, when you and your siblings got older, your mother came to you and your siblings and asked you all to

MERCEDES JOHNSON

forgive her, but it is hard for you to find it in your heart to forgive her. When you were younger, you will cry yourself to sleep saying over and over, "Love doesn't hurt like this." You told yourself over and over that when you got old enough, you were going to leave and never look back, and you promised yourself that you will never treat your kids the way your mother treated you and your siblings. But I want you to look again. No matter what your mother brought you and your siblings through, turn around and look again. In life, we only get one mother and father, and I know all that you had to go through was hard, but guess what, you didn't die, you actually made it through all the hell that you went through, and most importantly, your pain and struggles has made you stronger.

So what do I mean when I say look again? I mean simply that turn from your anger and unforgiveness and go back to your mother and tell her that you forgive her. Let me tell you that your

HERSTORY BREAKING THROUGH DARKNESS

forgiveness is tied to your healing and happiness. You have walked through life unhappy and carrying this burden, but I challenge and dare you on this day that you take control of your life and turn and look again and forgive your mother and be free from the spirit of unforgiveness and bitterness.

****

This addiction did not just start with my Mama. Oh no, honey. This came from a line of generations. This addiction started with my great- great- parents on both my mother and father's side. This addiction did not happen and start with my great-great- grandparents and stopped there. This addiction lingered for generations on both sides of my family. The beginning of this addiction is the result of poverty in the projects. And if not, specifically the Robert Taylor Projects, there was another way poverty introduced itself to my great-great- grandparents.

Within my early ages, every person I came across in the projects were alcoholics. I not only watched Mama

MERCEDES JOHNSON

from my family struggle with this addiction, but I remember watching Mama's mother struggle with this same addiction. Granny seemed more like a professional when it came to drinking. I swear there were times when I will watch her drink all day without taking a nap or anything. I mean she literally drank all day with and without my Mama. Their favorite drink they drank together was white port and Kool-Aid. I will watch them, and I remember trying to understand why my granny drank with Mama. I thought that was the weirdest thing ever, especially because I didn't want Mama to drink. I thought that more than anything my granny shouldn't have been condoning Mama alcohol addiction. But I guess when you too are addicted, there isn't much you can say to the next person.

    There were times when my granny lived with Mama and I. I loved my granny so for the most part of her living with us was fun. But I realized that when she stayed with us, her and Mama drank so much together. There were some nights when the two of them would stay up to the wee hours of the night drinking, listening to oldies, and reminiscing. As harmless and peaceful this might sound, I strongly despised it and hated it. I loved that Mama and my granny was bonding, but I hated that they felt like they could only bond over a drink. I hated their addiction, but I loved them beyond words.

It's funny how the very thing you hate, sooner or later you become. There was one specific night I sat under my granny while she drank, and I looked at her and asked her how and why she started drinking.

She answered me with her head tilted to the side, "Jada. I use to hate people that drink. I couldn't stand an alcoholic. When your mama and your auntie and uncles were younger, I would have them walk on the opposite side of the street when I would see an alcoholic. I didn't even want to walk on the same side of the street as them."

MERCEDES JOHNSON

As tears rolled down her cheeks, she said, "Now I'm one of them".

I felt my granny pain that night. I don't know exactly what I felt, but I know knots began to bald up in the center of stomach. I wanted to double over and scream because the pain was so severe. Instead of crying and showing the pain on my face, I sat there trying to be strong for granny. I watched her as she continued to drink her beer while her tears fell from her eyes. I sat still trying to hold back my tears the best way I knew how. I had to be strong for her. This was not my time to be weak or show any emotions. I had to be strong one.

Listen, do not allow your pride to cause you to fall in the very same ditch that you have looked down on other people for falling into. The same ditch that you have tried to avoid, and you talked about others who have fallen into have your name on it, and if you don't change your way of thinking, you too like my

HERSTORY BREAKING THROUGH DARKNESS

granny, will become a victim to the thing you hated. I hear the spirit of the Lord saying you have boasted yourself on your accomplishments in life and because you have made it out of the hood or projects, you feel like you are better than those who are still trapped and stuck. Your attitude is so bad that you won't dare bend down to help another person to get up from their place of misery and hurt. You have spent so much time living behind your own deceptive glasses that you can't even see when someone next to you is down or need your help. Whoever this is for, and if this is you, consider this a warning, get yourself together and change your way of thinking because your way of thinking is going to cause you to fall in a ditch/ pit that you never thought you would be in. I bind that spirit of pride right now in the mighty name of Jesus. I break it at its root now. I call it forth. I demand for it to take its grip off of you now in the mighty name of Jesus. I break that spirit of affectation. Listen whoever this is for you have been living

MERCEDES JOHNSON

in this fairytale life; people look at your life and think that you have it made and think that you are always happy and that you don't want for nothing. But that is a lie. Your life has been a lie. You are not happy. You are not living the life that you pretend to live before your peers. I break that spirit of affectation now in the mighty name of Jesus. I break that spirit of delusion in the name of Jesus. I bind that unclean spirit right now. I break it. That spirit of manipulation that has been hovering over your mind and speaking into your ears. I break it now. I call forth the power of the Holy Ghost to over take that lying and unclean spirit that has been lying to you and binding your mind to bondage. I break it. I break that bondage. I dig deep in your spirit, and I remove every corruptible seed that has been planted in you from your childhood. I remove every lie that has been spoken over your life. I remove them now. The lie of people telling you that would never be anything, and now you are living your life trying to prove people wrong. I break that people-pleasing spirit off your life right now in the mighty name of Jesus.

    I feel a breaking in my spirit right now. I feel a breaking, and I hear your spirit crying right now. You are thinking that finally someone sees you for you and understand you for you. Though you have lived your life hoping that no one sees your flaws, but on the inside, you were crying out and battling with yourself because apart of you want to be vulnerable and guarded at the same time. I get it, you are afraid of people seeing you for who you really are. You are afraid of people looking at you different since they have had this fabricated outlook on you, but listen to me in order to break this mask and living of pretense, you must become real with yourself. What I mean by being real with you is by simply admitting truth to yourself, allowing yourself to feel. See, sometimes when we live a life of pretend we will do whatever it take to keep our mind off of our reality, and one of the ways we do that is by shutting down our feelings and emotions by either constantly staying busy with work or education, or drinking and smoking. The mask has to be confronted, exposed and brought down. Second, after you are comfortable with being real and vulnerable with yourself, you should find one person, (hopefully someone of the same sex) whom you can take your mask off in front of as well as be vulnerable.

I pray for your healing and deliverance from your past and emotional hurts and pain. I want to advise you to seek healing and Godly counsel. Listen, if you don't allow healing and deliverance to take place, you will continue to live this life of affectation and pride, and it will eventually lead you into a ditch that you never thought you would fall into. Get healed and delivered now.

****

As you can see,

HERSTORY BREAKING THROUGH DARKNESS

alcoholics ran in my family really bad. And it did not just stop with my granny and Mama. My granny had six children altogether. One of her boys died a couple days after she gave birth to him. He actually died in Mama's arms when she was a child. I know that messed Mama up. With the death of my uncle that left my granny with five children alive, and as I hate to say this, but all five of them turned to liquor, and before they knew it, they all were addicted and were considered alcoholics. My father's side of the family was no different from Mama's side. Throughout my father's family line, there were alcoholics as well, including my grandmother, my father, uncle, great uncles, and great aunts.

    I did not only come from a line of alcoholics but drug dealers, drug users, thieves, and manipulators; depression, sexual immorality, sexual perversion, poverty, rebellion and many other seeds that connected itself to me as a child.

MERCEDES JOHNSON

See it wasn't my fault that my upbringing was not the best and it is not your fault either, but you don't have to make it your present or future. I had every reason to be worse off than I already was. When I say I should've been jacked up I am not exaggerating, but I am speaking the truth.

As stated in the section before, Mama was young when she had me. Mama had an addiction before and after she had me. Mama went through some life-threatening situations. Though Mama was going through so much on the inside, she tried her best to be strong for me. Mama might not have know how to show me love the way that I needed to be shown, but she tried by buying me every name brand shoe and clothing article that came out.

2
Material Isn't Enough I Need Love

~ ~ ~ ~

MAMA MADE SURE she kept me in the newest Jordans, filas, FUBUs, Guess, and every other name brand there was. Some people might say I had all I wanted, and Mama kept me sharp, and I didn't have to ask for anything. To an extent, they were right, but the very thing that was missing remained missing. No matter how many name brand clothes and shoes I got, no matter how many Nintendo 64 systems I got to occupy my time, it never replaced the quality time I desired to spend with Mama. Material possession did not fill the emptiness I felt as a child. The sad thing about this is the fact that Mama didn't see it, and if she did, she

MERCEDES JOHNSON

didn't make it her concern. And I can't blame her because she was raising me the best way she knew how. She didn't grow up with a silver spoon in her mouth. She didn't grow up with mommy and daddy. She grew up with the absence of the same exact love I was longing for as a child. Instead of receiving that love, she too longed for from her parents; my granny and her became more like best friends and drinking buddies. Love existed, but the emptiness, longing, hurt, pain and rejection remained dormant in Mama's heart.

Just because Mama gave birth to me it did not mean she was ready to be a mother. Though mama did grown-up things, it did not mean that the little girl that has been looking for love from a father did no longer exist anymore. It might have been easy for Mama to cover up the hurt and pain that she carried in her heart for years by drinking, partying and fighting, but it still remained. Mama never shared with me about the absence of her father, but it was noticeable. I will talk about how the absence of her father affected not just her life but my life as well.

    Before I move on, I want to tell a parent right now that is reading this book, I want to encourage you, woman of God, as I concluded the last sentence in the previous paragraph, I felt a tug in my spirit. I felt many mothers reading this some of you begun to see yourself in my mother's position. You began to feel bad and began to regret all the things you have put your children through. You didn't realize that your mistakes, your pain and hurt have affected your children. Some of you want to go to your children right now and apologize. I want to let you know that you are not alone, and I feel you right now, but let me tell you something, I did not write this book for you to live in regret. I come against that spirit of regret right now in the mighty name of Jesus. I have written this book to reveal these hidden seeds that lies dormant in your heart. By all means, woman of God, I did not write this to make

MERCEDES JOHNSON

you feel like an awful mother, but once again, I have written this for your deliverance and breakthrough. So even now, I pray that our Father touch your heart and remove the hardness and replace it with a heart of flesh right now in the mighty name of Jesus. I send the power of restoration to your family, life and home even now. I remove every stain and stench of bitterness, unforgiveness, division, heartbreak, selfishness, stubbornness, ill-spoken words, word curses, rejection, depression, oppression, hatred, resentment, offense, pity, pride, jealousy, isolation, intimidation, lies, vengeances, envy, regret, and heaviness. I break every generational curse off your immediate and long distance family right now in the mighty name of Jesus. With the power and authority that is invested in me, I decree and declare that restoration and freedom is getting ready to hit your home and your heart right now. Every chain that once separated you and your family is now broken, and restoration is taking place right now. I silence the voice of the enemy in your mind right now. I reverse the lies that have told you over and over that your children will never forgive you and the lies that have told you that you didn't do anything wrong to them, and they owe you an apology. I bind that lying serpent of division and pride right now, and I send fire to its messenger right now in the name of Jesus. Division will no longer rest between you and your family no longer after this day. Restoration, freedom and breakthrough are coming to your house and family *now*. In Jesus name. Amen!

MERCEDES JOHNSON

3
Bigger Than Us Lets Go Back
~ ~ ~ ~

REMEMBER I TOLD you all that I was going to go back and explain how the absence of my mother father affected not only her life, but my life as well. Like I have stated numerous times before that Mama and Daddy had me when the two of them were in their early teenage years.

HERSTORY BREAKING THROUGH DARKNESS

Let me recap that Mama and Daddy had me out of wedlock, and they was not faithful to one another. In the beginning, they were crazy about each other just like any other young couple that was looking for love. Their love story didn't last long, and hatred took the place in Mama's heart where "love" once lived toward Daddy. Since I was the outcome and result of their love act, I got the blows of hatred that mama felt toward Daddy.

Lets' rewind to the beginning when my granny gave birth to Mama. Their stories aren't a lot different from one another's. Granny was young when she had Mama. Mama was the third child and the second girl out of six children. Out of the six kids, my granny gave birth to Mama and her brother directly under her was the only two who shared the same father.

They all, just like me, was born out of wedlock. My grandfather was not in the lives of Mama or my uncle. He left my granny and got married and began to take care of his wife's daughter and son as if they were his own. So Mama, along with all her other siblings, grew up without their fathers in their lives. She just didn't grow up without a father, but her father was absent from her life. As sad as this might sound, I only speak the truth; the absence of a father was normal and was portrayed as if it was okay. But it was not okay, not then and not now. It affected not only Mama, but me as well.

Listen, mothers, please, please, please stop telling your sons and daughters that they don't need their fathers. Stop telling them that you are the only father that they need. That is not of God, and it is not Biblical. Matter of fact, that is a lie from Satan himself. Mothers, you are made and formed to be a mother and a nurturer, not a father. Being a father was not and will never be the role of a mother. I do understand that some of you are single mothers and that is understandable, but the seed that you are planting in your children is a lie and will bring about hurt and lies toward their father and men. Don't place your burdens and beliefs on your children.

With the absence of Mama's father and the emotional disconnection of her mother, Mama turned to liquor, tobacco and drugs along with sex. She was searching for something to fill the void that she was missing in her life. The fact that what was abnormal became normal to her; she couldn't recognize what it was that she was missing in her life. Since she couldn't put her finger on it, she went through many stages in her life, and sad to say, most of the stages that Mama went through eventually caused her downfall and bondage. Her pain, hurt, depression, misunderstanding, and anger was bigger than her, and they eventually led her to places and acts that she never thought she'll find herself in.

After Mama and my dad separated, that didn't stop Mama from looking for love to fill the void and holes in her broken heart. Though she carried bitterness and hatred toward Daddy, she still believed that love existed somewhere for her.

Earlier in the first section, I introduced you all to Mama's boyfriend Marcus. I know the way I described their encounters, you all would have thought that Mama and him was in a long-term relationship, but believe it or not, their relationship wasn't as serious as the others I witnessed. I guess the depths and levels of fighting they had, I too looked at their relationship equal as the others. But the difference from Marcus and the other two relationships I will introduce to you all is the length of the pain Mama and I endured together.

After Marcus, Mama met a young man by the name of Charles. Charles was older than Marcus. I don't think he was a lot older, but I do know that he was older. Just like Marcus, Charles was a drug dealer. The difference from these two was that Charles opened up shop right in the apartment as well as outside, meaning he did his dirty work in the house. Mama helped him out when he wasn't at the house when people came looking for work, and she would serve them.

When Charles came in the picture, he stayed around a lot longer than Marcus. In the beginning of Mama and Charles relationship, I actually thought that the two of them was doing well. Mama appeared to be happy and she stayed occupied with Charles. I was happy to see Mama smile and enjoy her relationship.

They rarely argued, and if they did, it was very minor. I was convinced that he was the one for Mama. Though he was young and sold drugs, he didn't bring drama and pain to our life. He was alright with me. But you know how people say what happens in the dark will eventually come to the light? Well, that proverb eventually came true for Charles.

Before I go any further, allow me to say I don't take

MERCEDES JOHNSON

back the fact that he was a nice young man. Mama was happy with him, and since she was happy so was I. But I understood something from watching him and Mama's relationship- sometimes what seem to be sweet can turn out bitter.

Like I stated in the beginning, Charles was a drug dealer, and he sometimes sold out and inside the house. He basically had a whole store in the house, and when he wasn't there Mama sold for him. With that being said, money was coming in and out the house. I guess to keep a woman happy, you have to be a breadwinner, and from the looks of things, that's what he was doing.

Allow me to go back to what I have learned from Mama and Charles's relationship. Okay, Charles was well known in the streets as well as in the projects. His name was ringing, and it didn't take long until someone will try to test him. Him and Mama were doing well, so I thought. Somewhere in Mama's spare time, she was seeing another guy. She never brought me around him or vice versa. I didn't even know she was messing around on Charles. I know you all might be thinking well how I know she was messing with another guy. Wait. Wait. I'm getting there.

One morning, Charles, Mama and I were in the living room lying down watching movies. Mama and Charles were on the couch while I was on the floor with my blankets, sheets and pillows. We slept in the living room the night before talking, laughing, play fighting and watching movies. I remember lying there when all of a sudden, there was a knock on the door. I remember the knock was light at first. It was so light that Mama or Charles did not hear it. The knock came again, and this time it was a little louder, but it wasn't rough sounding. I remember Charles got up from the couch and walked over to the door.

"Who is it?"

MERCEDES JOHNSON

There was a silence; nobody said a word.

"Who is it?"

Now remember we had a chain on the door, and there was a peephole. The doors in the projects were not your ordinary doors. These doors were extremely heavy.

Charles was still in front of the door when someone knocked briefly on the door a third time. This time, instead of saying who is it, Charles slightly cracked the door open. Wrong move. When he cracked the door open, the only thing Mama and I saw was the door being kicked open, the door smashing on Charles foot, him falling backwards, and men with ski masks and handguns swarmed our apartment. To my memory, I believe there were four to five men with ski masks and guns.

It all happened so fast. I couldn't believe my eyes. All I could do was stare at the men and hope that Mama and I was going to be okay. I was beyond scared. I was terrified. More than

HERSTORY BREAKING THROUGH DARKNESS

anything. I wanted it to be over. I tried closing my eyes hoping that when I opened them the men would be gone, but when I opened them, they were still there.

The men were everywhere throughout our two-bedroom apartment. All the men were scattered instead of one young man. I believe he was the ringleader of the group because he was calling out orders to the men while he stayed in the living room with us. With one surprisingly move, he swiftly took off his ski mask and smiled at Mama. We watched him as he walked over to the television in the living room and took a cigarette from Mama's Newport box. He lit his cigarette and came back to where we was sitting and began to talk directly to Mama.

"Where is the money and drugs?" he asked with no emotion in his voice. His voice sounded ice cold that sent chills down my spine.

Mama didn't move. She didn't even part her lips to release any words out of her mouth. She remained silent as

MERCEDES JOHNSON

if she was not moved by the coldness and stillness of his voice. Just as he stared at her with such a cold look in his eyes, Mama returned the same look.

I couldn't believe my eyes. I couldn't believe Mama behaved in such manner. But she did and she was.

Without warning, he walked over to where I was, sitting on the floor, still on my blankets and sheets; he quickly took out his gun and placed it at my temple. I felt the coldness of the cold silver metal gun placed on my head. I don't know if I was scared because my thoughts was so scattered. My thoughts were everywhere. Though my thoughts were all over the place, my body was still and numb.

I closed my eyes and said to myself, "Mama, you better open your mouth and tell this man all that he wants to know and tell him now." I was scared out of my mind. I have never had a gun pointed to my head. For crying out loud, I was still a child- a kid to be exact.

HERSTORY BREAKING THROUGH DARKNESS

What felt like hours of silence did not last longer than a second. Suddenly, I heard Mama's voice break the silence in the room; I heard Mama giving him directions to the money and drugs. As Mama gave him directions, he repeated everything back to his partners who were running around tearing up our apartment like it was nobody's business.

With those direct directions, they all went to where Mama told them the drugs and money were. Everybody in the apartment knew when the men found the "jackpot" as they called it, yelling went throughout the apartment. The men yelled out to their leader who was still in the living room with us. "We found it," they cried out with excitement. When he heard those words, a smirk appeared across his face as he looked at Mama.

Just as fast as they rushed in our apartment and took all the money and drugs Charles and Mama had stored up, all of them disappeared out the door, down the porch, and

MERCEDES JOHNSON

out the building. I don't know if Charles was scared or what, but throughout that whole time, he didn't say anything or move a muscle. He was so quiet it scared me. We all remained in our same position for at least about five minutes before Mama got up and headed straight to her room in the back. I heard Mama mumbling and rummaging through things in her room while Charles still sat there, I guess, in amazement or pure terror.

Mama came back in the living room telling Charles that they took their stash from the room as well. I guess the stash in their room was money that they hid aside from the other money they hid in the kitchen. Mama was livid. Before this day, I have never heard Mama use as many cuss words at one time, but boy oh boy, she was off the charts with them. Neither Charles nor I tried to calm Mama down. I wasn't trying to step into the fire and get burnt by trying to put it out.

The sad thing about

HERSTORY BREAKING THROUGH DARKNESS

this was the fact that when you are selling drugs and you get robbed, you cannot call the police and tell them you got robbed. Calling the police would be like telling on yourself, and that's one thing you don't do in the projects or in the drug gang. You don't call the police no matter what. If anything, you handle things on your own the best way you know how. No matter the cost and outcome, you must take matters into your own hands.

After the robbery took place, things began to unfold and skeletons began to come out the closet. It wasn't long after the robbery that Charles talked Mama into moving to Minnesota with him and his family. I guess he felt like moving to Minnesota was a lot better than Chicago. I don't know how exactly he got Mama to say yes to leave Chicago, but he did.

I don't remember much of the process that took place during the transitioning from Chicago to Minnesota. But I do remember how our life shifted from having our

MERCEDES JOHNSON

own home, room and food to sharing and living with people we did not know. I hated it. I couldn't believe Mama agreed to move to a whole new state with people we did not know.

I remember during the beginning of our stay in cold Minnesota, I stayed to myself. Mama could barely get me to utter out more than ten words at a time. I guess I was going through a stage of depression and isolation at the time. I felt lonely, and I wanted to go back to Chicago.

During these times, I guess Mama and Charles was happy together. He spent one half of his day arousing Mama's feeling and emotions and the other half searching for jobs. There were days when I would watch Charles and Mama from afar and wonder if he was showing Mama the amount of affection and attention to get her mind off of our current situations. Whatever he was doing was clearly working because Mama walked around smiling, giggling and drinking. It didn't take

HERSTORY BREAKING THROUGH DARKNESS

Charles long to get a job, and eventually, we moved out of Charles's family house into our own house.

Usually, one would be happy to know that they no longer had to share rooms with others, but I wasn't. It wasn't because I didn't developed such an amazing relationship with them, it's because I did enjoy their company. The kids was fun, funny and we actually called one another family, but despite that, there still remained a thirst and a hunger inside of me that not even the kids my own age could fulfill, and I tell you, I had an amazing time with them.

I feel strongly prompt to say this. Parents, please do not reject your children. I tell you from experience, you have no idea the type of damage you are doing to them. Not only the damage that is being done to them emotionally, but as well spiritually. Rejection is one of the number one things that open up the door for Satan to come in and torment a child's mind at a young age. Seeds of deception,

MERCEDES JOHNSON

hurt, rejection, anger, depression, and many others sit in the mind, emotions and spirit of your child. Children need their parent's attention, appraisal, approval and love. They desire words of affection from their parents especially from their mothers. I am not stating that the love of our father is less important than our mother because it is not. However, I do understand that it is the mother that carries the child in her womb for nine months. During that time, there is a bond that is created between the mother and the child. And sadly to say, the first form of rejection that a child experiences is the rejection from the mother, the father, or both parents. This type of rejection makes a child feel unloved, unwanted, undeserving, abandoned, hurt, unworthy, mistaken, unaccepted, alone, and the list goes on. A child cannot comprehend why their mother or father doesn't like to spend time with them, why their mother or father have time to spend with their friends, but when it comes to them, they don't have the time.

HERSTORY BREAKING THROUGH DARKNESS

Rather, it seem like this is small, and that they are just kids; they too have feelings, and they desire the attention of their parents more than anything. Matter of fact, it is at these times when a child is most vulnerable and innocent. They hunger for their parent's attention, approval, smile, hug, touch and words of encouragement.

Another thing that is so critical about these times when a child is vulnerable and innocent is that these are the times when Satan comes in and snatch their innocence by either rape, molestation, deception (through imaginary friends that is actually spirits that connect themselves to the child); imaginary friends comes through a child's imagination when the child has been rejected, pushed away, ignored, abandoned, isolated and lonely. Satan plays on these things and steals the purity and innocence of a child at an early age.

Parents, I warn you and charge you to evaluate yourself truthfully. I don't care how old your child or children may be right now, but if you have rejected them in any way, I charge you to ask them to forgive you for rejecting them and making them feel like a castaway. I also charge you to forgive yourself. Sometimes, we can do something without the knowledge that we are doing it. I know from experience that some people in general reject others without knowing that they have done so. However, truth be told, it doesn't matter if you did not know that you was rejecting your child during the time, and even if you were aware of rejecting your child (ren), that as well does not matter right now. What matters is that repentance, forgiveness, deliverance and healing take place so that broken relationships are mended and love is restored. I, guarantee you, no matter how old your child might be, questions of why his or her parents never loved them, what did they do to make their parents abandoned them, etc., still remains. I don't care how old they get until these questions and feelings are addressed, and forgiveness take place; these thoughts will torment their mind for the rest of their life. It will forever torment their mind and emotions because of the simple fact that the one person that was supposed to love them, accept them, care for them, and be there for them was the same person that did the opposite. The rejection of a parent leaves the deepest scars.

Before I move on, I want to imply once again that I do not say these things to make any parent feel bad. I do not bring any condemnation to any parent in any form possible. However, I do bring light to expose the tactics that Satan has used to bring division amongst mothers and daughters, fathers and sons, sister and sisters, etc. Rejection can come in many different forms; it can come from a parent showing favoritism toward the eldest or youngest child. This type of rejection can birth hatred and rivals between siblings, rebellion, drug abuse, self-harm and many others because the need of love and acceptance was

MERCEDES JOHNSON

not in the house. This type of rejection also causes one to run away from home at an early age, get involved in drugs, gangs, sexual acts such as homosexuality, lesbianism, pornography, prostitution or over indulgence in sex. It is easy to get entangled in these things when one is not receiving the love and acceptance that is needed at home.

I say all these things in order to shed light on broken relationships. The root of many relationships especially between a mother or father and their children is rejection. What seemed to be so little was actually something really big that has been tormenting your child(ren). But you, as well as a parent, has been struggling with the thoughts of where you went wrong with your kids and why they act like they don't like being around you. You struggle with these thoughts every night. There are times when you even cry yourself to sleep in hopes that one day you and your children will have the relationship that you and your parents never had. You too are being tormented, but you are too prideful and stubborn to ask your children for forgiveness. I plead with you, don't treat your children how your parents treated you. Break this curse of rejection by admitting to your children your mistakes and ask them for forgiveness. Whether they receive it right then and there or not, it does not matter. Your acts of obedience are all that matter, and God will do everything else. Amen.

  Back to what I was saying about the thirst and hunger that was deeply in me that the kids my age could not fill. Like I stated, most kids would have been happy that they finally had their own room again, but I wasn't happy. I mean, I guess seeing Mama happy made me happy, but it wasn't my own happiness.

  When we moved to our first small home, it was different, but nice. In Chicago, we didn't live in a house. Matter of fact, this was my first time ever seeing a house. I was used to seeing project buildings, not houses. I

MERCEDES JOHNSON

remember in the house we had an upstairs, downstairs and an attic. More than anything about the house, I remember the attic the most because that's where I spent most of my time when I was home from school. Mama bought me a doll when we moved to our house. I remember when I would come home from school, I would grab my baby doll and head to the attic for hours, playing and talking to my doll. When I would get tired of my playing with my doll, I would do word search puzzles for hours at a time until I fell asleep. Mama couldn't understand why I spent so much time in the attic by myself. I guess, by this time, I got used to being by myself. I embraced the lifestyle of isolation if you will. Truth is, I was tired of watching Mama drink all day everyday. I hated the sight of liquor. I hated it with everything in me. I didn't want to continue watching Mama slowly kill herself because of this toxic poison. I loved Mama, but I hated the one thing that she loved. She refused to stop, and I refused to watch.

HERSTORY BREAKING THROUGH DARKNESS

It didn't take long after moving into our own home for the arguing and fighting to happen between Mama and Charles. There were a lot of things as a child that I got use to, like for instance Mama's drinking. Though I hated it, I got use to it by locking myself in the attic and either playing with my doll or doing crossword puzzles. But I could never get use to Mama and Charles fighting. That was one thing I couldn't pretend that did not bother me. I loved Mama too much to stand back and watch or listen to a man put their hands on her. I don't know which one was worse- witnessing someone trying to have sex with your mother when she is too drunk to feel someone taking advantage of her, or witnessing a man harming her physically. I would say both of them was traumatizing, but more than anything, I believe watching men time after time physically abuse Mama traumatized me mentally more than the other one.

To some people, they probably would have gotten

MERCEDES JOHNSON

use to it because the fighting with Charles and Mama increased, not to mention the other men I have witnessed Mama fight with. So this was not new to me, but I don't think violence is something that a child could ever get comfortable with. I could never get comfortable with hearing Mama and Charles yelling, and myself running to the living room where they were with tears running down my face and my heart pounding against my chest because, in the back of my mind, I already knew that they were fighting.

No matter how many times I witnessed Mama fighting, I could never get use to it, and I don't believe I should have. I was terrified. There were many times I was right in the midst of them fighting, screaming and begging them to stop. I would bang on Charles as hard and fast as I could. I just wanted him to stop hitting her. I wanted it to end. I wanted them to stop fighting. I couldn't understand why love made people act in such way. Every man Mama was with, they fought. With different men, the fighting styles were different; some lasted longer than others. Mama had control in some, and others, she didn't. They all were different, but they all affected me in the same way.

It wasn't long until Charles was on my hate list. I developed hatred toward him just as I developed hatred toward Daddy, alcohol, and everything else that either brought a separation between Mama and I or brought us hurt and pain. My dad did not really fit in the category with bringing separation between Mama and I, but since mama hated him, I developed hatred towards him as well. Charles made his way to the hate list without even knowing it. The first time I witnessed him putting his hands on Mama was the beginning when all respect for him was out the window, and hatred replaced the respect I once had toward him.

****

Reader, if you have been carefully following along

MERCEDES JOHNSON

with me, you would have picked up so far that hatred filled my heart at a young age. I haven't hit my years of eight yet. So far, all that you have experienced with me have occurred seven years old and younger. If I can point this out for any parent who is reading this, all these things that I have witnessed wasn't because of my mistakes or my choices, but I was reaping the consequences of the generations that was before me. I say generations because everything didn't just start with Mama as I explained before with the drinking, but these things were generational, and they were passed down from one generation to the next.

    I developed hatred towards men as you can see because of what I witnessed Mama go through with men. Every man she was with would beat her. Mama was far from a punk; she didn't just sit there and let them beat on her. Best believe she fought back and at the end of some of the fights, she came out on top, but that is not the point. In the eyes of a young fragile girl who depended on her mother and all she knew was her mother, seeing any person not just a man, but also any person doing harm to her mother birthed a form of hate toward men and whoever else after while. My outlook on men was distorted and negative. At a young age, I made up in my mind that I hated all men. They were never to be trusted in my eyes or with my heart.

Reader, keep in mind as you are reading this, remember that I made this declaration before I turned eight years old.

I want you to remember these seeds, (the seeds of hatred, rejection, poverty, hurt, bitterness, alcohol, etc.) because I want you to see and understand the effect of seeds (words). A seed is planted no matter how old the person maybe, and no matter when the seed is planted, there is always fruit that bear the fruit of that seed from years ago.

MERCEDES JOHNSON

4
Tried In The Fire
~ ~ ~ ~

THE FIGHTING GOT worse between Charles and Mama. As the fighting got worse between the two of them, Mama's consumption of liquor intake increased. It wasn't long until Mama smile slowly disappeared. I began to see Mama fall back into a state depression. Her glow disappeared, and it was evident that she wasn't happy. She didn't try to pretend like she was happy. As she drank, I stayed in the attic away from her. I played with my doll, trying my best to take my mind off Mama. I knew she was

HERSTORY BREAKING THROUGH DARKNESS

hurting. I felt it. I felt her pain, and it ached my bones.

I never understood just how connected mama and I were, and neither did she. I carried the weight and burden of her pain. Mama didn't have to tell me when she was hurt, I would feel it before she reacted to it. The pain she would feel would ache my very bones. It would get so bad to the point I will crawl on my knees to Mama because I would not be able to walk. Mama would try her best to stop the pain. As I got older, I understood that whenever Mama fail in depression the aches would come. I carried Mama's weight and pain without knowing it.

I watched Charles and Mama drift apart. I watched Mama drown in her depression and beer. I felt her pain, but I remained silent. Never saying a word. There was so much tension in the air and anger everywhere. More than anything, I had built up anger and wanted to run away from our despair. I just wanted to go back to Chicago. I hated being some place that neither Mama nor I wasn't happy,

MERCEDES JOHNSON

but I dared not tell Mama that. I continued to pretend.

I remember one specific day, I'm not sure if we still had our own place or if this was a time when we were living with one of Charles family member's. As you can see, our living situation was pretty unstable. This particular day, Mama decided to drink throughout the whole day, and by time it got later in the hour, Mama was pretty tore up. On this day in particular, Mama put me in bed early, and she stayed up doing her usual- listening to music, drinking and crying.

Usually, Mama would drink herself to sleep, but this day was different. Instead of going to sleep, Mama decided that she would cook herself something to eat. Mama started her food, but before the food got done, she was passed out. The liquor got the best of her.

As stated before, Mama put me to in bed early this day. I had no idea what was going on. The room where I was sleeping was up stairs.

HERSTORY BREAKING THROUGH DARKNESS

If I am not mistaken, the house we were in was a two or three-level bedroom house.

I was startled out of my sleep, and to my surprise, I was awakened to flames of fire surrounding me.

"Mom, Mom," screams came forth from the pit of my stomach through my mouth. I tried looking around the room, but my eyes quickly began to get heavy and burned from the smoke. I couldn't see through the clouds of smoke. Before I knew it, my neighbors somehow found a way in my room. They got me out of our house and brought me to theirs. I looked around and immediately began to panic.

"Where's my mama? Where's my mama?" tears instantly began to build up in my throat. I was no longer asking them to tell me where Mama was, but I was demanding an answer from them. The door behind me slammed, and I turned around and saw Mama.

Without thinking, I ran to Mama with tears rushing

MERCEDES JOHNSON

down my face. I threw my shaking body against her and wrapped my arms around her. I held tightly around Mama's waist for dear life. I didn't want to let her go. I was too afraid. At this very moment, I realized how much I not only needed Mama, but how my heart yearned and beat for her.

Mama and I didn't speak about the fire that night. We slept over at our neighbor's house until the very next morning. We got up early in the morning and began cleaning and wiping down the walls of our house. While cleaning, Mama yelled out to me from across of the room.

"Yes ma'am," I yelled back to Mama.

"Come here."

I placed the towel in the bucket of hot soapy water and walked over to where Mama was located.

"Yes, ma'am," I stood standing before mama with a big smile spread across my bright face.

Mama stared at me with an identical smile on her face as mine. I loved when

HERSTORY BREAKING THROUGH DARKNESS

Mama smiled. She not only smiled to show her teeth, but Mama also smiled with her eyes. Her smile was so bright that it brought joy and happiness to those around her. She was amazing.

"I love you," Mama said while staring in my eyes.

"I love you too, Mom," I said while embracing her leg.

"Look at me," Mama gently grabbed my arm and removed me from her leg so that she can get a better look at me.

"Don't say anything about what happen last night okay?"

I looked at Mama and saw the seriousness in her face and eyes. "Yes, ma'am," I replied, reflecting the same seriousness she gave me.

For the remaining of the day, we cleaned and painted the house. I obeyed Mama and never made mention of the fire. I never really did understand why Mama never wanted to talk about it, but for whatever reason she kept it to herself. I was just given the orders to keep my mouth shut. I knew better to question Mama's decisions and reasoning of things. I understood that my place as her child was to obey without asking questions. Mama established the principle, "A child stays in a child place," and it was never my place to question Mama's decisions about anything.

I took heed to everything Mama said to me; though there was many things as a child I did not agree with, I remained obedient to Mama. I say this because as a child, I took everything Mama showed and told me as truth. However, as I got older, I began to realize that some things that Mama made me to keep as a family secret grew as a stumbling block and hindrance in my life as I got older.

Many of you who are reading this, (especially mothers), you all are thinking how was this possible. To your knowledge and

HERSTORY BREAKING THROUGH DARKNESS

capability, you have raised your children the best way you know how. Some of the ways you have raised your children was based on your own upbringing, with the fear of seeing your child(ren) go through the same things you yourself have went through as a child. With this type of mentality of raising your child(ren), it may have caused some of you to spoil your children, neglect them or even abuse them.

With Mama, she tried raising me the best way she knew how. She tried giving me everything that she did not have. But one crucial thing is when one is empty, it is hard to give someone something they don't have. See, I needed more of Mama. As a child, I needed her undivided attention. I needed the words of affirmation from her. I needed her to validate me. The very things I needed as a child from her, she was not able to give because she was never given these things as a child. Once again, when one is empty it is hard to give someone something that they don't have. Mama couldn't give me what I needed because

MERCEDES JOHNSON

she didn't have it.

    I feel like someone needed to know that. Someone needs to understand that you can no longer walk around hating your mother for not being the mother that you wish and desired her to be. You cannot walk around with the unforgiveness that has been lying heavily upon your heart. This anger, bitterness, resentment, hurt, and unforgiveness you have been harboring in your heart toward your mother have been tormenting you. I hear you saying by the spirit of God, what do I mean when I say, "tormenting" you. It means that for many years, the anger, hurt, pain and resentment you have held in your heart toward your mother has grown. There is something in you that reminds you daily of how hurt you are. You are not only reminded of your hurt, but inside of you, there's an uproaring of anger that comes. This anger that lies on the inside of you has grown over the years into hatred, bitterness and resentment. There's a part of you that

HERSTORY BREAKING THROUGH DARKNESS

still question why and how your mother treated you the way that she did. Everyday, you are being tormented by the things that your mother lacked, and the very thing that she lacked as a parent is the very thing that you needed from her. But I want to challenge you on this day; I want you to think about the proverb I gave earlier. When a person is empty themselves it is hard for them to give someone something that they themselves did not have. I want you to think about your mother upbringing. I want you to take this reality into consideration. I am not saying that it was okay for you to have gone through what have gone through due to the lack of love from your mother, but I want you to be free from unforgiveness that have been tormenting you for years.

****

Father, I pray for your children who are reading this book. I pray for the crying and weeping soul that has been convicted by reading this part of the book. Father, I lift

MERCEDES JOHNSON

them up before you now. Father, I pray that from this very moment, you continue to touch your children's heart and bring about such a conviction that will cause them to confess their sins and repent. Father, I pray as you continue to press on their heart and bring your children to repentance, that you will fill them up with your unconditional love. Father, I pray that your love overcomes every form of anger, resentment, unforgiveness, pride, selfishness, stubbornness, hurt, rejection and rebellion. I apply the blood of Jesus over every person who is reading this. I apply the blood of Jesus over your minds, homes, spirits, souls, families, and finances. I place a hedge of protection over and around you, and I speak unity into your spirit in the name of Jesus. Amen.

  Mama taught me at a young age to speak only when spoken to, and if you are not spoken to, don't open your mouth. I took this principle to heart and learned how to be a master of disguise at a young age. I knew how to pretend like everything was okay, even when they weren't. But I didn't learn this on my own. I developed this habit from the many times Mama made me remain quiet. Mama taught me how to pretend and act like everything was fine when in reality everything around us would be a disaster. The house fire was no different. Though the fire wasn't severe and life threatening, Mama made me shut my mouth about it and never to bring it up again.

Over time, secrets soon catch up with you, and the thing that you were trying to keep a secret eventually exposes itself. I learned as a child that a person could only pretend for so long until the mask will be confronted by the individual who is wearing the mask, or the mask will be confronted by someone else; either way it will be exposed.

"Speak only when spoken to," I can't recall how many times Mama said this to me either in front of her friends or in private. This was Mama's favorite line and principle she taught me early on. A child speaks only when spoken to; if not spoken to, you remain silent. As a child, you are to stay out of grown folks' conversations. A child stay in a child's place and that's it and that's all. I never questioned Mama' decision or the way she did things. I understood her concepts, and even if I didn't understand them or agree with them, I obeyed Mama and what was told of me. However, this concept that Mama branded in me not only made me obey her, but it also placed a muffler on my mouth. It caused me to hold back on a lot of things. It caused me to shut down in a way of communication because I never exposed anything that bothered me; I allowed things to build up because I took Mama's way of disciplining to heart.

    Many of you are reading this and thinking that I took this concept of discipline too far. Many of you don't understand where I am coming from because your parents have said the same words

HERSTORY BREAKING THROUGH DARKNESS

to you. Before I go any further, allow me to say that I understand the concept, but what I want to bring to the forefront is how it affected me as a child even within my adult years.

    I have a question, what happens when you are never asked as a child how was your day in school? What happens as a child when you are never addressed with questions or conversations that involves your thoughts, opinions or concerns? What happen when all of your childhood life, you been told numerous of times to speak only when spoken to and you await for the day or moment for mama, daddy, granny, aunt, uncle, cousin, somebody ask you how you are doing? What happens when fear of speaking grips the mind and heart of a child because they are afraid of being disciplined? What happens?

    Well let me tell you what happens, that child goes into isolation. Why? Because that child feel like they are not worthy, unimportant and invisible. How do I know

MERCEDES JOHNSON

this? How can I say this confidently? This was my situation, better yet my life. "Speak when spoken to," these words constantly beat across the conscious of my mind. What happens when you obey this concept of discipline and the time or day never comes when you are spoken to?

This was branded within me so much to the point that I remained silent and never spoke. I covered up my hurt, my pain and my own concerns. There were times when I wanted to speak. There were times when I wanted to cry and express how I was feeling, but didn't know how. I didn't know how to say when something or someone was hurting me because I wasn't taught how. Mama spent more time disciplining me on what not to do, but never took the time teaching me what to do.

What may seem to be common sense for one individual isn't common sense across the board. Some people have to be taught, and what you are not taught by adults, you soon learn

HERSTORY BREAKING THROUGH DARKNESS

through life struggles and experiences.

There's a proverb that goes on in most families, and the proverbs goes like this: "Whatever goes on in this house/ family stays in this house," meaning our family business stays between our families, it doesn't have anything to do with anybody else.

What I hated the most about this proverb is that this type of mentality has created secrets within families. This creates dysfunctions within families. This creates division within families. Why? Because no one never speak up on things, and everyone walks around like things never happen. But what happens when Uncle, Granddad or Dad walks around touching on his grandchildren, nieces, nephews or children and everyone knows it, but no one says anything? And what makes it even worse is the fact that the children are not the only ones who has been touched, but the mothers, aunties and uncles too have been touched when they were younger, but no one talks about it.

MERCEDES JOHNSON

Everyone wants to act like it never happened. Everyone wants to act like the family is okay and perfect on the outside, but in reality, everybody is strung out on drugs, alcohol, pornography, etc., because when they were younger, they were told, "Whatever goes on in the house/family stay in this family," but I have question. What if the family secret is the very thing that is causing torment, hurt, pain and addictions to one's life because it was installed in them as a child to never voice what was going on, and when they do, everyone ignores them? This is a form of a generational curse that could be broken if the muffler is taken off one's mouth.

****

Father, in the mighty name of Jesus, I snatch away the muffler from your children's mouth. I release a spirit of boldness upon every individual that has had their voice stolen from them as a child. I release their voice box now in the mighty name of Jesus. I

HERSTORY BREAKING THROUGH DARKNESS

decree and declare that they will no longer be a victim and prisoner to their childhood terrors any longer. I break such spells off their mind now in the mighty name of Jesus. I break such a spirit of shame, embarrassment, guilt, manipulation, and control off your mind now in the mighty name of Jesus. I break your mind from such a prison now. I release you from every form of cultural bondage right now. I declare that you are not what people have spoken over your life as a child. I break that word curse now in the mighty name of Jesus. I declare freedom over your mind. I break off every limitation off your mind and your spirit man now. I declare that you no longer have to live up to the standards of mama, daddy, friends, grandma, aunts or uncles. I release you from such bondage of people pleasing in the mighty name of Jesus. I release your spirit from their influence in the mighty name of Jesus. I declare for your spirit to be free. I declare for you to arise. Arise from such a pit. Arise from such bondage. Arise and spread your wings in the mighty name of Jesus. You are more than a conqueror. You can do all things through Christ who strengthen you. I encourage you to press pass all the accusations. Press through all the naysayers, lift up your head, and claim your victory and walk in it. Take the muffler off and free yourself in the matchless name of Jesus. Amen.

WOLVES IN SHEEP CLOTHING

MERCEDES JOHNSON

1
SMOOTH OPERATOR
~ ~ ~ ~

WHAT DOESN'T KILL can only make you stronger. That's what I was told. "Jada, toughen up." "Jada, stop all that crying, you're not dead," "Jada, what doesn't kill you can only make you stronger, so dry your eyes and suck it up."

I wasn't supposed to have feelings and emotions, and if so, I sure wasn't suppose to show them. So little ole me, sweet, quiet, innocent Jada held everything inside. No one knew what I was dealing with because I was a child. Since I was a child, I didn't have nerves. Since I was a child, I didn't go through things. Oh how that was a lie

HERSTORY BREAKING THROUGH DARKNESS

from Satan himself.

If someone would have taken the time to ask me, "Jada how are you feeling?" "Jada, what's on your mind, I see that you have been more quiet and isolated more than before?" If someone, just someone, showed me attention or a sense of care, they would have caught on to the fact that sweet ole, innocent, quiet Jada was slowly losing herself to a false identity.

What was I to do? What was I to say? Who would have listened? Maybe it was my fault. Maybe I was wrong. Yes, I was wrong. Yes, I was wrong. I was the cause and blame for everything that was happening to me. I can't tell anyone. What would they think about me? What would they say about me? Jada, you are fast and a little whore, that's what they would have said without thinking twice about it.

These thoughts, words, voices and accusations raced continually in my young mind; this was my battlefield of the mind. My identity and innocence was

MERCEDES JOHNSON

being snatched right before my eyes.

See, he was smooth as butter and dark as chocolate. He was tall like Morris and bald like Chestnut. Words of affirmation rolled off his tongue like the dew of honey. He was smooth and not to mention sharp as a shiny thumb tap. He had it altogether. Who would have dared allowed Mister to walk past without looking twice in the direction of the cool of his expensive cologne. Mister was not only a smooth operator, but he was the smooth operator.

"Jada," I jumped out of my sleep to Mama calling my name. Before getting out the bed, I wiped the sleep out of my eyes and slowly began to make my way out my bedroom door. While making my way to the bathroom, my thoughts began to roam. I wondered what it is Mama wanted with me. As my thoughts began to roam, I hurriedly took care of my personal hygiene. I was anxious to see what it was that Mama wanted with me.

"Yes, ma'am," I replied to Mama calling

me.

When I met Mama in the kitchen, I noticed that she was not alone. I stood in the doorway of the kitchen and watched Mama giggle in the presence of this man whom I have never seen in the projects before. I watched how Mama looked into his eyes as his smooth words drew her into his web. As they talked, this stranger man held Mama's undivided attention.

I stood at the doorway of the kitchen and watched Mama and this stranger interact. I never saw Mama look or act this way. It almost felt like I was watching the little girl in Mama take place of the adult. I also noticed something different about this strange man, something very different from every other man Mama brought to the house. He was much older than Mama. This was the first time Mama brought an older man to the house. I watched, and my curiosity rose to its limit.

"Hey, Mama," I said as I entered into the kitchen. I

MERCEDES JOHNSON

couldn't help but to eye this stranger up and down.

"Hey baby," Mama said, wrapping me in her arms and kissing me on my forehead and cheeks. Mama's juicy kisses took my mind off the stranger and placed them on Mama.

"Stop, stop, stop," I said screaming, squirming and trying to wiggle out of Mama's arms. The more I tried running away, the tighter Mama held on to me.

Before I could move my face, Mama sloppily and playfully continued kissing all over my face. As much as I yelled for Mama to stop, I enjoyed her attention more than anything. This went on for what felt like ten or fifteen minutes. Eventually, it came to an end, and when it did, I didn't want it to stop.

Mama scooped me up in her arms and placed me on her lap. By this time, I was sitting across the table from the stranger. Reality hit me immediately, and I remembered the reasoning of Mama calling for me to come to her, and it was to meet the strange man. The smile that once was displayed across my face was completely gone, and I looked directly at the strange man who looked back at me with a huge smile on his face that showed all of his top and bottom teeth.

I just stared at him, and the more I stared, the more he looked at me with a smile on his face. I couldn't help but to notice a difference about this strange man than the other men Mama brought around. Yes, he was older than the other men, but that wasn't it.

Mama eventually broke the silence, "Baby, I want you to meet someone," Mama said while removing me from her lap." I stood there with my arms across my chest. "This is Mister," Mama said while trying to ignore the attitude I was giving off.

Mister, I thought to myself, what type of name is that? Why would his mother name him Mister? What was she thinking or was she even thinking? I didn't know how

MERCEDES JOHNSON

to respond to Mama introducing me to Mister. I didn't know how to receive him. The truth is, I was afraid to receive him because I was afraid for Mama. I didn't want him to hurt her. I didn't want him to leave her. I didn't want to see Mama in pain anymore.

It wasn't easy for me to trust men. I watched too many men walk in and out of our lives. I watched too many men make Mama cry. I watched silently as the tears streaked down my stiff and heated face. Though I never said anything to Mama, I saw everything from the arguing to the fighting, the many nights Mama stayed up in the middle of the nights crying and drinking. It was too much to witness. The pain was overbearing and overwhelming.

I didn't know Mister, or anything about him. But what I did know was that he was a man who had Mama's full attention, and I did not like it or him.

I knew that this wasn't going to be the first or the last time seeing Mister.

HERSTORY BREAKING THROUGH DARKNESS

Mama displayed a liking for him more than she has ever had for any other man she dated.

As the days and weeks went by, Mama would come in my room giddy and bubbly. "Jada, put some clothes on and not just any clothes, but your pretty girlie clothes we are about to go."

"Yes, ma'am," I responded under my breath. I wasn't dumb. I knew Mama and I were getting ready to go meet Mister somewhere. I never understood why Mama had me come along because they paid me no attention. Mama sent me off to play alone while the two of them sat around laughing and drinking for hours at a time. I hated being out with them because we was always outside, and I had to use the restroom every fifteen minutes, and Mama would make me urinate outside. I hated it, and Mama knew it, but she did not care. She would say, "Jada, you better squat, wipe and shake." I should have known, Mama was going to say that, that was her motto when using the

MERCEDES JOHNSON

restroom outside. No matter how many times Mama had me do it, it was just something I could never get use to, but it was either that or peeing on myself and Mama was not having that. I knew better to not to get on Mama's nerves. I learned quickly to do as I was told, with no questions asked.

It never failed when we met up with Mister, he would either have a brown paper bag or a white plastic bag, and inside the bag would be a fifty-cent juice, multiple quarter bags of chips, packs of quarter bags of little Debbie cakes, and candy in his hand. He greeted Mama with his arms stretched out with a grin plastered across his face. I slowly walked behind Mama with my chin touching my chest. Mama paid me no attention by this time. She was wrapped up in Mister's arms and being drowned in the repetitive kisses over her face. I watched in disgust, as Mama seemed to melt in his arms.

By this time, I

HERSTORY BREAKING THROUGH DARKNESS

completely removed myself from them and went off in the school park in lot and jumped rope by myself. As I jumped rope, Mama and Mister sat on the stairs of DuSable High School and drank their beer and talked. It didn't take long until Mama called me over to where her and Mister were sitting. Already knowing and having Mister's routine memorized, I walked over to them slowly. When I finally made my way over to them, Mama held the plastic bag dangling from her hand, and her can of beer in the other hand. Without saying anything, I took the bag from Mama's hand and began to walk away.

"What's your problem? Come back over here and give me that bag back."

Walking back over there with tears rolling down my face. I handed Mama the bag of snacks.

"What's your problem and I'm not going to ask you again," Mama said, this time looking directly in my eyes.

Slowly wiping my tears from my face, "Nothing," I

MERCEDES JOHNSON

said in a half whisper.

"Jada, stop playing with me. Why are you crying? Didn't nobody do anything to you."

"You're yelling at me," I said, covering my face with my trembling hands.

"Girl, nobody yelling at you. You're not that sensitive. You already know I don't play. When someone gives you something, you say thank you or if you don't want it you say no thank you. That of what you just pulled don't fly with me and you know it. Now if you got an attitude, you can go back over there and try it again, but all that crying and sensitive stuff save it for it another day."

Without fully realizing, I felt embarrassed and instantly, my embarrassment turned to anger. Surprisingly, my anger was not toward Mama, but it was toward Mister. I wished that he disappeared. I wished that he never brought the candy. It was because of him that Mama yelled at me. At this point, I didn't want the candy any more. I didn't want anything that he had to offer, but I knew if I rejected it, Mama would've thought I was trying to show out, and there's nobody that can show out better than her. I didn't want a whooping in front of Mister, so I walked over to him and slurred my words as I said, "Thank you, Mister, for the candy."

These types of outings with Mister did not last long until he started showing up at the house more frequently. His frequent visits went from one day out the week to two days, and eventually, he was bringing bags of clothes over weekly. He went from coming over in the mornings and leaving in the evening to coming over in the morning and staying until the next day. Before I knew it, Mister had his side of the room and Mama had her side of the room. He not only came over to visit, but he eventually moved in. He was not only a friend of Mama's anymore, but he was Mama's man.

It took some getting use to with Mister because

MERCEDES JOHNSON

Mama haven't had a man live with us since we had left Minnesota and Charles behind us, so Mister was hard to embrace wholly. But I watched closely how Mama and Mister spent a lot of time together. I watched how Mama introduced Mister to all of her friends with such a bright smile across her face. I have to admit, I had never saw this type of glow on Mama before. She was so happy to show him off not only to her friends, but to the family as well. Everyone accepted him and liked him. It wasn't as easy for me to openly accept him like everyone else did. It took more observance. I needed to know and wanted to know his agenda that he had. I needed to know what he wanted from Mama.

    To my surprise, Mister stayed around a lot longer than I expected and thought. Not only did he stay around longer, he kept a smile on Mama face. Though he drank and smoked cigarettes a lot, I was happy to see Mama happy. I had no choice but

HERSTORY BREAKING THROUGH DARKNESS

to respect him. My respect for Mister eventually turned into a liking and welcoming.

MERCEDES JOHNSON

2
Same Tune Different Step
~ ~ ~ ~

I COULD HAVE been the one that was in the dark and didn't know what was going on or maybe all of us.

A year has passed by and Mama and Mister were still going strong. He was still keeping Mama happy, and he was keeping me laughing. It felt good to have a dad in the house. Mister and I developed a strong bond, a father-daughter relationship. Wherever he went, I went. He was my dad, and I was his daughter.

As Mister and Mama's relationship grew, I noticed the slight tension and mini- arguments they would have behind close doors. It wasn't long until Mama's smile slowly began to dwindle away. I didn't know what was going on because they didn't display their problems out in the open. Well, it started that way. Surprisingly, I was okay with there mini-disputes because it wasn't affecting Mama too much to the point of staying up in the middle of the night crying and drinking. So I figured whatever it was, it couldn't be that bad. So I thought.

Listen, ya'll everything that look good on the outside can be poison and rotten on the inside. Everything that glitters isn't gold, okay. I have witnessed as a child Mama go through heartache after heartache. I don't know why God is taking me this way, but I want to encourage some women, mothers in general. The way you allow a man to handle you, talk to you, and treat you in front of your kids does not only affect you, but it will affect your children in the long run. Your daughter will either grow up hating you for allowing a man to treat you the way they did, or she will grow up with hate and no respect toward men, or she'll grow up thinking that the way you were

MERCEDES JOHNSON

treated is okay, and that cycle will continue.

****

As a mouthpiece of God, I close every door that has been opened for any form of domestic abuse. I break physical abuse now in the mighty name of Jesus. I break emotional abuse in the mighty name of Jesus. I break financial and mental abuse right now in the mighty name of Jesus. I break every word curse that was spoken over your life by a boyfriend, by an ex, and by every male species. I break that word curse now in the mighty name of Jesus. I break your mind free from such a bondage and stronghold now in the mighty name of Jesus. I decree as a Prophet of God that you are not what men have said and treated you as. I declare over your spirit that you are a queen and not a whore. You are beautiful, you are precious, and you are worth more than you have been treated. I break you free from such a weight of low self-esteem. I break your mind free from such a barrier and

HERSTORY BREAKING THROUGH DARKNESS

heaviness now in the name of Jesus. Mother, I break the feeling of guilt off you now in the mighty name of Jesus. I break that lie that has made you feel like your children will not forgive you so you find yourself going out of your way to gain their approval and forgiveness, but today I break such a spirit of manipulation off your mind now in the mighty name of Jesus. I release you from such a prison. I release the blood of Jesus over your mind, your spirit and your soul now. I break every form of bondage now. I break every lie that has built strongholds pertaining to how you look and think about yourself. I break such a lie now in the mighty name of Jesus. I loose you, woman of God. I loose you now. I loose your mind from the mindset of always needing to be in a relationship. I break such a spirit that's call codependence. I break that Ahab spirit now in the mighty name of Jesus. I release strength over your mind. I release the strength of the Holy Ghost over you now, woman of God. I declare your freedom in the mighty name

MERCEDES JOHNSON

of Jesus. Amen.

****

I remember one day coming home from school Mama was in her room, and she was yelling and cussing someone out on the other side of the phone. I don't know who it was, but whoever it was, Mama was letting them have it. I bypassed her door and headed to the refrigerator, grabbed a lunchable, went into my room, and turned to nickelodeon. On this particular day, I decided to stay in my room instead of going outside. Mama and I barely talked, I stayed in my room, and she was in and out the house. Later on that night, after dinner, I was in my room getting prepared for bed when I heard someone knocking on the door. I figured it couldn't be anybody but Mister because he hasn't been home all day.

"Who is it?" Mama said as she dragged her feet across the tile floors.

"Mister."

HERSTORY BREAKING THROUGH DARKNESS

"Hold on," Mama said with an attitude. She made him stand out in the hallway for what seemed like five minutes. When mama decided to open the door, I heard the front door slam then her bedroom door.

"What's wrong with you?" I heard Mister ask Mama nervously.

"Oh, nothing," Mama responded sarcastically.

"Yo, for real," Mister said in a more serious tone.

I never heard Mister use that tone of voice with Mama before so I knew whatever was going on was serious. Mister always seemed cool, calm and collected. There were times when Mama would say little slick stuff to get to him or under his skin, and he would either ignore her or laugh at her. Mister was a real smooth operator, and for the most part, he stayed to himself. The days when Mama would go out with her friends to have drinks, Mister would stay in the house, and we would watch television while he drank his beer, and I ate my original flavored David

MERCEDES JOHNSON

sunflower seeds.

    I pressed my ear up to the wall in order to hear Mama and Mister. Silence fell in the room they were in. I stood there with my ear to the wall, shaking in my skin. I wondered what Mister did to Mama. Suddenly, I heard Mama speaking really low and soft. I couldn't make out if she was crying or what. Mister began mumbling to Mama. I stranded to hear what they were saying. Finally, I heard the word *wife*.

    My mouth swung wide open as my ear was plastered to the wall. I couldn't believe what I was hearing. I didn't want to believe it. I couldn't believe it. Mister was family; now he was my dad. I even heard him and Mama have several talks about getting married. This couldn't be true. Mister couldn't have had another family, let alone married to someone.

    I didn't know what Mama and I was going to do. We were already attached.

HERSTORY BREAKING THROUGH DARKNESS

We let him into our family. He was a part of the family. As mad as I wanted to be at Mister, I couldn't bring myself to be angry with him because I loved him as my dad. That night, I laid down wondering what Mama was going to do. I wondered if we were going to say goodbye to Mister.

As the days, weeks and months passed by, I began to wonder if I was the crazy one, or if I was the one hearing things. Mama and Mister acted as if they didn't have a conversation about him being married, having a wife, and another family. They walked around like everything was fine, but I noticed the distance that was coming between them. Mister was still always at the house; we all continued to watch movies together and ate dinner as a "family," but I could feel the difference. I notice the distant glare in Mama's eyes. It was a glare of hopelessness or disappointment.

I noticed Mama stayed on the phone arguing back and forth with Mister's wife. I guess Mister figured since

MERCEDES JOHNSON

the both of them knew about one another, he didn't have to pretend anymore. He would go days without coming home to Mama and that would make Mama sick. She will blow up Mister's wife phone cussing her out. I started to think that they all were enjoying it because whenever Mister would be at our house, his wife would call Mama and tell her how Mister was over there and vice versa. But I noticed Mister never stepped in and said too much of anything. Though his face would be distorted with irritation and frustration, he never opened his mouth to interject.

I don't know when and how, but somewhere down the line, Mama accepted the fact that Mister had a wife and family, and she was okay with it. Maybe deep down, she didn't like it, but she never left him, and he didn't leave her. Everything in me figured that it probably was wrong, but I didn't know any better, and all I was concerned about was having *my* dad around.

It amazed me how

HERSTORY BREAKING THROUGH DARKNESS

close Mister and I grew. There were days when Mama and him would get into arguments because Mama would either yell at me or whoop me, and Mister would step in to defend me, but that didn't last long. Mama didn't play when it came to disciplining me; she didn't allow for anyone to step in to try to teach her parenting skills, not even her own mother.

MERCEDES JOHNSON

3
One Plus One Equals One
~ ~ ~ ~

ONE YEAR TURNED to two years then three. That which was kept a secret was now revealed; the cat was out the bag. The names of little boys and girls that had Mister's last name behind their first name remained mysterious faces. Everyone knew of one another, their house and my house, but no one officially met face-to-face yet.

What would seem weird and uncomfortable to another family was embraced and accepted by our family. I remember Mama walking into my room and took a seat on the bed. "Hey, Jada," Mama said with her hands in my hair.

"Hi, Mom." Smiling from ear to ear.

"Today, your dad is going to bring your brother and sister over here so ya'll can play and meet each other." I know I wasn't the brightest child, but I wasn't dumb by far. When Mama said my brother and sister I thought to myself, *I don't ever remember Mama having any more kids at the time.* I know my real dad had another daughter, but we didn't see each other a lot because she lived in another area. I sat there looking at Mama with my eyes searching her face, and her expression never changed.

"Okay," I said, with a smile plastered across my face.

Hours later, I heard the front door open and slam shut and then I heard Mister talking, "Baby, take your shoes off right here. The restroom is right there down the hall. Okay, wait, let me get your sister situated then I'll

MERCEDES JOHNSON

show you everything else."

Due to the many voices and whispering in the apartment, I realized that Mister was talking to his children. I was happy that they were here. I was so excited. I jumped out the bed then jumped back in. I didn't know if I should have ran out the room and greet them with a hug or stay in my room and wait until they came in. I battled until the door crept open and a dark smooth face poked in and out really fast. I heard tiny whispers and giggles on the other side of my room door.

"Jada," Mister called my name playfully.

I jumped out the bed really fast, wiping my face as if I was in a deep sleep. I slowly opened the door to find a dark-skinned girl and boy standing outside my room door with a wide smile plastered across their face.

"Hi, sister," they both said in unison. I was taken by surprise. My thoughts began to roam immediately. *"Ya'll do know that I am not ya'll sister. Do ya'll know that Mister been cheating on ya'll mama with my mama. The nights ya'll papa haven't been coming home is because he been here with me and my mama."*

I was brought back to reality by Mister voice, "Jada."

Without thinking, I hurriedly placed both of my hands over my face. I tried hiding my smile and my laughter. I don't know why I was so tickled, but I was. Mister grabbed me and swept me up in his arms and lifted me over his shoulders, twirling me around in the hallway really fast.

"Stop, stop, stop," I screamed and laughed at the top of my lungs.

Mister playfully slammed on the floor and punched and stomped me playfully. I laid on the floor balled up screaming and laughing. Before I knew it, he threw his daughter then his son on top of me. We all were in the

MERCEDES JOHNSON

hallway screaming, "No," "Stop." Laughter and screams filled the whole apartment for what felt like twenty minutes.

Eventually, the fun came to an end, and introduction came in play. We all got up from the floor and started to run toward Mister before he put up his hand and said stop. We all froze where we were standing and began laughing.

Mister waited patiently and quietly on us to get ourselves together. "Are ya'll done?" he asked, looking directly at us with a smile on his face.

We all just looked at him without responding to his question. "Good," he said.

"Jada, this is your sister Dajah. Dajah, this is your sister Jada." Before Mister could introduce me to his son, Dajah ran to me and wrapped her arms around me and gave me the biggest hug ever.

"Let her go, stupid," I heard Mister's son yell in the background. I figured

HERSTORY BREAKING THROUGH DARKNESS

Dajah was the youngest amongst the two of them.

When Dajah let me go, her brother walked up to me. "What up, sis, I'm your brother Mario." We hugged, and the introduction was over.

We all ran into my room, played and talked like we have known each other for years. They were so comfortable with talking to me it was almost scary. I grew up with Mama telling me, "Just because someone smiles or wave at you, that doesn't mean that they are your friends." I figured their Mama didn't raise them the same as Mama raised me.

Dajah was the talkative one while Mario criticized everything she said and did. I noticed through conversation Mario was portraying to be mature in front of me. I watched as he shut down everything Dajah said. They couldn't have been that much far apart in age. If anything, they were no more than three years apart and no less than two.

Dajah ran and out of the room, knocking on the

door where Mama and Mister were. I heard her crying and reporting to Mister everything Mario had said and done to her. I looked at Mario from the corner of my eyes, and his body posture changed and softened up instantly.

"No she lying dad," Mario yelled from the room as he got up and made his way out the door to where Mister, mama and Dajah were.

I laid in my bed with my eyes closed listening to Dajah and Mario yell back and forth at one another. Mister allowed them to yell at one another until he stepped in and spoke to Mario with power and force behind his voice. In the beginning, Mario tried to go back and forth with his dad, but that was his biggest mistake; Mister wasn't having it. He shut that down as fast as it started. Before I knew it, I heard Mario crying and whining trying to plea his case. No matter how much he wanted Mister to hear him out his plea and tears did him no justice. I noticed that Mister didn't play when it came to

HERSTORY BREAKING THROUGH DARKNESS

Dajah, and Mario was reaping what he had sown.

It wasn't long until the two of them came back into the room. Dajah came in with a smile so bright as the sun on her dark skinned round face. Her innocent joy and excitement brought a smile upon my face. I looked at her and thought to myself, *How can someone not love such a young innocent soul as hers?*

I opened my eyes to Dajah sitting on the bed, looking down at me waiting to get my attention. She reminded me of a little sister that I never had. I slightly turned my head sideways and looked into her eyes. I saw hurt and pain deep in her eyes. It felt as if I was swimming in a pool of black coal, and the waves brought torment and horror. I wanted to ask her so bad what was it that brought her so much pain that made her feel like she couldn't escape.

Though I was young just like her, I wasn't naïve to pain and hurt. I knew them too well. For myself, I was fine

MERCEDES JOHNSON

with the pain and hurt that I dealt with, but when I saw another young person who was hurt it sparked anger within me.

Whatever it was, I knew it was deep, and she herself probably couldn't even identify the deep-rooted pain she was suffering and dealing with as a child.

I have learned growing up that children take on the burden of their parents. I not only learned that with Mama, but the night looking into Dajah's eyes. The pain she was dealing with was not of her own, but the weight of her parents. For crying out loud, her father was having an affair on her mother and everyone acted as if it was normal. They taught us to believe that it was okay, and there was nothing wrong with it. No matter how much Dajah and the rest of us grew to love each other as brothers and sisters, the truth remained that it birthed division amongst their family and confusion within our minds and hearts. It wasn't right.

To make matters

HERSTORY BREAKING THROUGH DARKNESS

worse, it became such a norm that their mother knew where Mister was bringing her children when he brought them to our house. Everybody was okay that this married man had another family outside of his marriage. There weren't any standards. I could imagine how Dajah and her other siblings felt. Their father was no longer in the house anymore, and when he was, it wasn't long because he spent his time with Mama and I.

I really feel this in my spirit. Parents, rather you realize it or not, children need a two- parent home. We need both of our parents in the home. We need our father just as much as we need our mother. I looked in that girl's eyes as a child myself and saw for myself what the division and separation done not just to their family, but also to her as a child. Though she may have never spoke up about it, it left a scar.

Every action that you make as parents affects your children whether good or bad. In this situation, the affect

MERCEDES JOHNSON

wasn't good, but we was taught that it was good. We were taught that nothing was wrong with what was going on. Why? Because her mother was cheating as well. The difference from her infidelity and Mister's was that she was cheating with multiple women. She was in a lesbian relationship. There's no telling how long she been in and out of relationships with women while married, but that is neither here or there the fact of the matter is that they both were in the wrong and didn't realize that they were not only destroying their marriage, but their children's perception on marriage.

It's bad enough to deal with your parents divorcing, but it's a different type of pain and confusion when both of your parents are openly cheating. When you are watching your mother bring other women to the house, and they are having lesbian relationships. If that's not bad enough, but as a child, you are witnessing your mother and father both having sexual intercourse

HERSTORY BREAKING THROUGH DARKNESS

with the women your mother is bringing home. This distorts a child's whole thought process and understanding of love and marriage as a whole. This opens the door for sexual perversion to enter into the heart, spirit and mind of a child at a young age because of what he or she has been exposed to.

We must guard our children. For it is when they are young that they are the most vulnerable and fragile.

What was different from Dajah's mom and Mama was that mama didn't play with the same sex relationships. Mama loved men too much so I never saw Mama involved sexually with another woman, but that didn't make Mama's wrongdoing any better or different than the other two. As I looked into Dajah's almond-shaped eyes, I could only imagine how she felt knowing that when she went home, she was going home to her mother with another woman. Not to mention it wasn't no better that when her dad brought her and Mario to my house, they were witnessing

MERCEDES JOHNSON

their father showing love and affection to another woman besides their mother.

Could you step outside of your own shoes right now and take a step in their shoes- matter of fact, our shoes? Could you imagine the thoughts that ran through our minds? Could you see the levels of confusion that stirred up in our mind? These are babies we are talking about that had to witness this. I hear in the spirit some of you are saying that you too had to deal with this when you were younger so what's the difference. See, you don't see the point of the whole thing, and you think I am making a big deal out of this, but, let me tell you, it does matter and it is a big deal. Let me tell you, why because even for you, though you are older and have kids, it's still hard for you to trust because you have seen so much infidelity between your mother and father, and now you don't know whom to trust, and lastly, you don't know how to authentically trust.

There's somebody

HERSTORY BREAKING THROUGH DARKNESS

that is reading this book, and you are being broken right now in a way that you have never being broken before. Yes, you have felt what it means to be broke "financially" as well as physically. You have experienced such a disconnection and rejection from your family as you got into your teenage years, and you could never understand why you always felt like the odd one and the black sheep of the family. As a child, you witnessed your father abuse your mother and your siblings. What first started off as petty disagreements and arguments led to verbal and physical abuse. The abuse eventually escalated to infidelity. You witnessed through nights of tears watching your father cheat on your mother and abuse her and your siblings. By you, being the oldest, you tried to be the strong one for your siblings, but that only lasted for so long.

Now you are on your fourth marriage, and you still aren't happy. You have tried to change the color of your finger nail polish. You have tried different hairstyles and

MERCEDES JOHNSON

colors. You have tried everything that you thought could help the inner-depth pain in your heart, but none of it helped.

The marriage that you are in now has helped you realize that there was nothing wrong with the men you were with before, but it was and still is you. It's the pain, bitterness, hurt, unforgiveness and distrust you have in your heart. You are probably thinking where did all this come from? Well, let me shine light to the dark place; it came from the infidelity you witnessed from your father as a little girl.

Your mother and father started their marriage very happy, and you all were happy. Many nights, you have wondered how and what made your father go from this perfect husband and father to you all's worst enemy. This has caused you to build walls in your heart. It is hard for you to trust men. You have bitterness instilled in your heart due to the hurt and pain from your father. Woman of God, I want to encourage you to think about seeing a licensed Christian counselor. You are broken and hurt, and you need to allow God to heal you from the hurt and pain you have experienced from your childhood.

I hear the Spirit of the Lord saying, "If you take this step of faith, everything that once held you down will no longer have a hold on you any longer." I hear the Spirit of the Lord saying, "There has been many nights you have waken up in the middle of the night with cold sweats, and you been wondering when will this ever come to an end. I hear the Spirit of the Lord saying, "The reason you have been getting attacked in your sleep is because of the hurt, bitterness and unforgiveness you are holding on to." I see in many of your dreams you are always being chased by something, and many of the times, you find yourself running either in a dark alley or down a dark street. While you are running, I see shadows popping up, and these

MERCEDES JOHNSON

shadows symbolize the people you thought was for you and some are family members. I see you running to some of these people, and as you run to them, they eventually turn to a foreign creature and begin to mimic you in laughter.

I hear the Spirit of the Lord saying, "The very things that you have been running from in your sleep is the very things you have been running from." I hear the Spirit of the Lord saying, "How long, how long are you going to run? When are you going to deal with it and face it?" I hear the Spirit of the Lord saying, "You can't run all of your life." There will come a time when the very things that you never wanted to talk about or deal with will eventually deal with you. I hear the Spirit of the Lord say, "It is time and I will be here to help you. No more running. No more running. No more running. I hear the Spirit of the Lord say, "Arise and shine, my child, for your light has come, and on this day, I have given you strength and power over every demonic force that have tried to take away your strength. I have come to give you strength. I have come to give you life and life more abundantly. You shall live and not die, thus saidth the Lord."

Before I go any further, I want to encourage someone else who is reading this book, I want to let you know that the Lord said, you have been wrestling with a decision, and this decision is pertaining to the relationship between you and your children. A couple of years ago, you allowed child protection to gain custody of your children. You have a baby boy and a girl whom you have not seen for close to two and half years. Before you read this book, you had no intentions of fighting for the custody of your children. Somewhere in the back of your mind, you felt as if it was too late. Guilt and doubt has settled in your mind and have had you believing that your children hated you and didn't want anything to do with you. But in the mighty name of Jesus, I declare war on the spirit of guilt and doubt

MERCEDES JOHNSON

right now in the mighty name of Jesus. I bind every lie that has spoken to keep you and your children separated. I bind it now in the mighty name of Jesus. I hear the Spirit of the Lord saying right now He is freeing your mind and spirit from every trap and snare of Satan's. By the power that is invested in me, I cleanse your spirit from the very residue of drugs right now in the mighty name of Jesus. I seduce proof your spirit now in the mighty name of Jesus. I cover you under the blood of Jesus right now. I hide you now in the blood of Jesus from every familiar spirit in the name of Jesus. I declare your freedom. I declare you free now in the mighty name of Jesus. Woman of God, by the power that is invested in me, I release you from this mental enslavement. I charge your spirit now to arise and go down to the court and figure out what you need to do in order to get your children back. Meet with your caseworker and come up with a strategic plan. I hear the Lord saying for the next ten weeks, you shall have favor

HERSTORY BREAKING THROUGH DARKNESS

with the court system, job resources, and housing, and building managers in Jesus name. Amen.

I hear the Spirit of the Lord saying for someone else, child of God this is not the time to give up. Woman of God, I hear and see you crying in your apartment at home by yourself. For many years growing up, you have told yourself that you would not treat your children the way your mother have treated you. You have gone out of your way to make sure your children would not want for anything. You have succeeded in this area materialistically as well as showering them with love and care. But I see you in this place where you are becoming tired and draining. You are beginning to look at families around you, and within some of these families, the fathers are still in the picture. I want to encourage you to keep moving forward and do not give up. Your children are watching you and seeing all that you are pouring into them, and they are very thankful for it. I hear the Lord saying, "Hold on just a little

MERCEDES JOHNSON

longer for it will pay off in the long run." I see a man coming into your life when your daughter enters into her teenage years. I see this man being all that you have desired and longed for in a man. I hear the Lord saying concerning this man here, he will not be just any man, but he will be your husband.

Woman of God, I also see that you are very particular when it comes to men. You have wondered why it's hard for you to find the right type of guy. Well, it is because you are different. I see that there have been times when you were willing to sacrifice your standards just to be in a relationship, but your love for your children didn't allow you to do it. I hear the Lord saying because you desire the best for your children and you love and sacrifice so much for them, the very things that you have asked God for, and sometimes you have thought that your prayer requests was too much or abnormal, but the Lord said you shall see them come into fruition in Jesus's name. The Lord said this is not your end, but this is only your beginning. Stay strong and don't give up for greater is not only hitting your life, but your home and family. I see your children going to the best schools and colleges. I hear the Lord say because of the love you have shown and poured unto your children the decisions that they make when they get older will be ordered by the love you have shown them. They shall not stray away or depart from your love or care. The Lord said your family shall be a close-knit family, and love shall be the center of it all. Your work is not in vain in Jesus name. Amen.

MERCEDES JOHNSON

4
When Sweetness Turns To Bitterness
~ ~ ~ ~

IF YOU HAVE ever had a mouth full of sour patch kids in your mouth, in the beginning, the candy is really sour, and you find yourself making funny faces due to the taste of the candy, but eventually, it goes from being sour and tart then sweet. We would call these sour patch kids bittersweet.

The RnB singer

HERSTORY BREAKING THROUGH DARKNESS

Avant wrote a song titled, "Don't Take Your Love Away." I'm pretty sure all of you know the song front to back even you who are saved, sanctified and Holy Ghost filled. Remember, you haven't been saved all your life, and even if you have brought up in the church, you too had your days when you didn't always listen to Praise and Worship music, I'm just saying. Anyways, there's a part of this song that really caught my attention every time I heard it. At first, I didn't understand what Avant was saying in this song or any other song of his, but his songs sounded good to my ears. However, as I started this part of the book, his song began to play in my head, not the whole song, but certain lyrics from the song. The lyrics goes like this:

> She said everything that that's
>
> Sweet ain't good for you, no
>
> And everything that glitters ain't gold

That brings back a tune for some of you. I know right. In the book of Matthew chapter 7, it states,

MERCEDES JOHNSON

You will know them by their fruits. Do men gather their grapes from thornbushes or figs from thistles? Even so, every good tree bears good fruit, but a bad tree bears bad fruit. A good tree cannot bear bad fruit, nor can a bad tree bear good fruit. (Matt 7:16-18, KJV).

Basically what these verses is saying, if you all will allow me to put a little slang in this, I will say that these verses is saying the same thing brother Avant was saying, "Everything that glitters ain't gold," in so many words, don't be fooled by one's outside appearance.

Now, over the time Mama and Mister being together, I mentioned that we too became really close. We got so close to the point I began to call him dad, and he identified me as his daughter. I loved Mister as my own father, though I knew that he wasn't, I wouldn't have traded him in for nothing in the world.

I believe I clung to Mister the way I did because he gave me the attention that my parents didn't. While my dad was spending time in the penitentiary and Mama was out drinking, Mister was in the house with me watching television, cooking and showing me the attention and love that every young person long for from their parents. Remember, my dad went to the penitentiary when I was four, so I didn't know what it felt like to actually have a father figure in the house until Mister came around.

    When Mister would bring Dajah and Mario around, he made sure he included me in everything. I didn't feel like a half-sister; matter of fact, I didn't know what half-siblings were until I got older. In our house, there wasn't any half this or half that; we all were family and that was that. No matter how dysfunctional things were Dajah, Mario and I loved when we were altogether. To us, we were biologically brothers and sisters.

    Mister and Mama's relationship wasn't the healthiest. They too just like the previous relationships

MERCEDES JOHNSON

Mama was involved in got into physical altercations, and just like the other ones, I found myself trying to break them up. What I noticed about Mister was that he was hesitant to fight and even argue back with Mama. It took a lot to make Mister angry with Mama, but when he got there, it wasn't no calming him down. Another thing I noticed Mister's reaction to Mama hitting him wasn't to immediately hit her back. He would try his hardest to pin her down and demand for her to stop, but if you knew anything about Mama, that didn't work but only added to the fuel.

Mister and Mama's relationship was like an emotional rollercoaster. They were up and down, sun and rain, joy and sorrow. Some days, Mama wanted Mister to stay in the house, and she argued with him up and down telling him that he couldn't go anywhere and how much she loved him and needed him. Then there were other days when Mama was rushing in and out of her room with black and white plastic bags

HERSTORY BREAKING THROUGH DARKNESS

tossing Mister clothes inside of the bags. During this time, Mister yelled throughout the apartment at Mama as she moved frantically as if his voice was not heard or didn't matter. This was the rollercoaster. Him and her arguments and fights lasted for hours and sometimes days.

Mister came in our lives in the shadow of an answered prayer. He appeared to be the perfect companionship for Mama and the perfect father for me. He was perfect in our eyes. But how many of you know that the devil can and will come in many forms. He will come to fulfill the desires of your flesh, and what may feel good to our flesh isn't always good for our spirit. Whenever we receive a gift from our enemy, the devil it will eventually come to an end. The Bible says, "The thief cometh not, but for to steal, and to kill, and to destroy: I (Jesus) am come that they might have life, and that they might have it more abundantly," (John 10:10). The devil comes to seek whom he may devour. He preys on the weak. When I say weak, I am not speaking only about physical weakness, but emotional, spiritual, financial, mental, relational, etc., the devil seeks to find a open area of weakness, and when he find that open wound, he sends something or someone to fill those voided areas, but it don't last long. See, the devil doesn't want you to be happy. He doesn't want you to be joyous. He doesn't want you to be free from those things that hurt, torment, pain and suffers you. He'll send a man your way to bind your eyes, which causes you to stay in that place you are in longer. So he binds your eyes with temporary medication. As a reminder, he does this to cause you to stay in the place of distress, brokenness, frustration and hardship. The most deceitful part about this is that one will not realize that they are still in this place because a man, woman, jobs, food, money, and drugs have distracted you.

I know many of you who are reading this can relate to this during one or more

HERSTORY BREAKING THROUGH DARKNESS

phases throughout your life. Some of you are in situations- friendships, jobs, relationships, churches- and states that you know God has been told you to depart yourself from. There's someone reading this, and I feel in my spirit that everything around you has been falling apart. You live in a city within the state of Texas. Last year, you felt a tug in your spirit to move from Texas, but you got comfortable there. Everything was going well for you, then out of nowhere, things slowly began to fall apart, and it started with your job. For the past six months, you have been diligently and angrily searching for a new job. Though you have been in this dry place for six months, you refuse to tell your family or friends that you need help. I hear the Spirit of the Lord saying, "You have gotten to a place and got too comfortable." You have gotten to a place where you felt like you didn't need anybody. You began to lean and depend on yourself and not Him. I hear the Spirit of the Lord saying, "You have become your own god." You have

MERCEDES JOHNSON

allowed pride to step into your life. But I hear God saying everything you are experiencing now is for your good. See, you had to be knocked down off your high horse, if God wouldn't have intervened at this time, you would have completely walked away from God. There was a job opportunity offered to you a while back and what you didn't know is that that particular job was going to lead you astray from God due to the amount of money they were willing to pay you. Now you feel like you don't have anything or anyone. You feel like you are alone, but I hear the Spirit of the Lord saying, "This is the place you need to be." You need to come back to Him. You need to know that He's your provider, and that without Him, you cannot make it. Without Him, you are nothing. I see that before you went to Texas, your relationship with God was really good. I see that during this time, you use to get up in the morning between 4:00 and 5:00a.m and pray. You had a life of prayer, but slowly you turned away due to the busyness of work and the distraction of the bonus checks and raises on your job. You forgot where your help have come from. I come against the lying tongue that has told you that God is punishing you. I bind that lie up now in the mighty name of Jesus. You are not being punished; you are being stripped and being brought down from your high place. God is calling you back to Him, and you know exactly who you are. Amen.

We all know that peaches aren't always sweet, and roses don't always smell good. Mister went from being a life savior to the devil himself. As I go headfirst into this section of the book, I would like to warn you now that you might want to fasten your seatbelt and put on the whole armor of God. This very issue and situation that is about to be exposed is very sensitive, and I want to caution you that if you have not dealt with this issue in your own life it is possible to cause something in you to rise up. But I want to say though it may rise up, I declare to you that it will no longer lie dormant, and by the time you are done reading this book, you will rise up, and take charge over every problem in your life. You, your family or anyone close to you will no longer be terrorized by things of the past. You will rise up and take back your freedom and happiness in the name of Jesus. Lastly I am not responsible for the prayer warriors, intercessors, worshippers, and prophetic voices that are going to rise up throughout the earth from this book, but I do encourage you to rise up and go full force without looking back. Let's start!

Valentine's Day, February 14 between the years of 1997 to 1999, Mama was in jail this particular Valentine's Day for fighting. Mister and I were in the living room sitting on the couch watching *Change of Hearts* falling immediately behind WWE when The Rock first started wrestling and absolutely everybody's favorite. Mister was sitting on the couch drinking his beer, and I was sitting directly under his arm. We

HERSTORY BREAKING THROUGH DARKNESS

sat there laughing and talking about how Mama loved The Rock, and how the Rock always raised his eyebrow. This laughter and giggles lasted for quite some time.

My eyelids closed shut as the night grew longer, and the dark clouds slowly covered the once shining sun. I didn't bother to get up and head to my bedroom. My restless body remained limp under Mister's heavy stature as he continued laughing at the television shows and drinking his cans of beer. I couldn't tell you how long I was passed out from exhaustion; I imagine it couldn't have been too long. As I slept there in a deep slumber, my sleep was interrupted with something wet, slightly warm, and moist brush gently across cheeks. I moved slowly under the sensation that first started from one spot on my cheek to my lips. I opened my eyes to find Mister heaving heavily over me, pressing his full body against my body, and his mouth completely covering mine. Our eyes locked as I starred in his eyes frantically as my frail and small body squirmed

MERCEDES JOHNSON

under his fully-grown body.

"I love you. I love you," Mister sloppily pressed his slimy wet lips against my ear and breathed heavily in my ear as he repeatedly told me how much he loved me. My young mind could not grasp what was going on. I couldn't detect how I was supposed to feel. For crying out loud I was no older than eight and no younger than six and all I was sure of at that time is that Mister loved me and he showed me the attention that Mama and Daddy didn't show me. Somehow, the more Mister whispered to me that he loved me over and over, his words seeped into my subconscious mind, and without registering everything that was taking place, I believed him.

This is how powerful words are and not only that but rejection. Mister manipulated me with telling me that he loved me, he made me think that what he was doing was an act of love. Due to me vulnerability and yearn of wanting to be loved and accepted, I thought he was showing me love.

See, when you are dealing with rejection, its like you have a void in your heart that's dying to be filled. Usually, when one is dealing with rejection, it typically stems from the absence of love or acceptance. Rejection doesn't have an age on it. It is very typical for a child to come out their mother's womb with rejection attached to them with many reasons, but one way for sure how rejection can connect to a child at birth is when the mother contemplate about aborting the child.

I am not saying all of this to divert from the situation with Mister; I will get back to that I feel like I am helping somebody right now. See, there are a lot of women who has been molested as a child, but they never tell the whole story of what took place so they never become truly free. I come against that spirit of shame now in the mighty name of Jesus. I hear in my spirit someone saying right now, what would people think of me if they knew that I

MERCEDES JOHNSON

began to enjoy what was happening? What would they think of me? What would they say? Honey, let me be the first to say this to you, welcome to the party because you are not the only one who not only found themselves enjoying this sexual perversion, there's thousands maybe even millions who has this same story, honey, you're not alone. I want to encourage you, don't beat yourself up. It was not your fault, sweetie. Many of you were too young to even fully comprehend what was going on. Yes, you could have said something at the time, but you didn't and guess what it still doesn't mean that what have happened to you was your fault. You were a baby. You were taken advantage of. Your mind and body was manipulated to think and feel that everything that was happening to you were okay.

Let me tell you all something, Valentine's Day was just the beginning, but it didn't stop there on the couch, and it didn't stop with just a

HERSTORY BREAKING THROUGH DARKNESS

kiss. My innocence was stripped and taken from me, and I didn't even know it. Let me tell you, Mister fondled with me so much that it became normal to me and let me remind you again that I was at least between the ages of six and eight years old, and this what I looked forward to. I was convinced that this was love. I believed that this was Mister's way to show me that he loved me, and believe it or not, my body began to crave and yearn for his touch.

    Listen, there are some of you whose reading this in complete disbelief and some who are disgusted, but I have learned that if I want to be free I have to tell the *whole* truth. See, right now this thing is bigger than me, and to be honest, it's not even about me, but it's about that young girl who has been molested half of her life by her uncle, and she is at her breaking point of giving up. This is about that young girl who is saying, if her dad or uncle comes in her room one more night, she's going to either take his life or her own life. This is about that young girl who hates herself

MERCEDES JOHNSON

because she listened to the devil tell her lies about what have happened to her as a child, and now she can't look at herself in the mirror. So as you can see, it is not about me, but it's about the next young girl who is going through the same thing. I'm here to tell you, sweetie, that I been where you are, and it is not your fault. You are not the blame.

With Mister, manipulation was a big factor. He didn't just tell me how much he loved me and needed me, but he went as far as telling me how I was his girlfriend and how one day he wanted to marry me. He performed oral sex on me for hours at a time. Listen, I couldn't have made this up even if I wanted to. I hear some of you thinking, where was my mom when all of this was taking place; she was either outside or sometimes in the other room laid out drunk. This was my life for almost two years nonstop.

Before I presume any further, I felt in my spirit to explain something to a mother or mothers who don't know what to do with their teenage daughter or preteen daughter who is very sexually. Mother, I feel your pain right now; you been trying to figure out if and how you have gone wrong with your daughter(s). For so long, you have been blaming yourself thinking that your parenting skills were bad. You been trying to figure out why your twelve, thirteen, fourteen and fifteen year old daughter(s) crave the attention from men the way that they do. You have watched how they have grown from such innocent young ladies into sex driven and promiscuous women. Mother, I see and feel your frustration; let me explain something to you in a deeper and spiritual sense in this spectrum. Let's look at sex as a whole. Biblically speaking, we know that God created sex within a marriage between man and woman. With this understanding, we know that sex is good as long as it is within marriage according to the Bible.

Driving a little deeper, there's many Scriptures that I can quote that state then such and such knew his wife then she bore a son. Whenever the Bible says, "And he knew his wife," it is speaking of sexual relations. Okay, let's go a little further the word *knew* means "intimacy and relations." When the Bible mentions this word, it is not speaking about it in the way we know it to be. We have to understand that we all are spirit beings. Genesis 1:26, "And God said, Let us make man in our image, after our likeness," this verse is speaking of our spirit man, not our physical man chapter two speaks about the physical man. Now that we have the understanding that we all our spiritual beings, when two spiritual beings come together and know one another in an intimate way "sexually," these two spirit beings becomes one. If we were to look at this in the spirit realm, every time we lay down with someone outside and within marriage we become one with that person.

Let me give you an example. Let's say that there's a guy by the name of JoJo, and JoJo grows up with an alcoholic abusive mother who will get drunk and beat him and his little sisters. JoJo never knew his father, and when little JoJo got older, he joined a gang and began using street drugs. Then we have little Vanessa who has been through similar things as JoJo, and these two young people meet, and they begin liking one another. Things start to move fast for the two, with a mixture of partying and drugs; JoJo and Vanessa takes the next step and he knew her, "sexually." Right at that very moment, Vanessa and JoJo becomes one within the spirit realm, and without knowledge, they create what we call a spiritual soul tie. Some of you are thinking what is a spiritual soul tie?

    Let's look at this a little further in the spirit realm when these two became intimate sexually; every burden, weight, depression, abuse, torment, addictions, etc. that JoJo was carrying in his spirit entered into Vanessa's spirit and vice versa, so in the spirit realm, the two of their spirits connected with one another, which created a bond, or in

MERCEDES JOHNSON

other words a spiritual covenant. So this is where we enter into spiritual soul ties. We now have a clear understanding and vivid picture that when two people have sex, their spirit beings come together as one, right?

I want you all to envision JoJo and Vanessa inside of an empty gym room. JoJo stands on the right side of the gym and Vanessa stands on the left side. Now both of them are holding a long cord or jump rope in their hand, which means the rope/ cord is stretched from one side of the gym to the opposite side. Now directly in the middle of this out stretched cord/ rope is a visible huge knot. While JoJo and Vanessa are holding onto their ends of the cord/rope, six people walk into the gym with them, but three of them walk to where JoJo is located in the gym and the other three walk to where Vanessa is located. The three people on the right side walked to the middle and grabbed hold of the knot, and the people on the left side did as the other three. While the six of them are in the

HERSTORY BREAKING THROUGH DARKNESS

middle holding on to the knot, JoJo and Vanessa remains standing on the opposite sides of the gym holding unto their ends of the rope/cord.

Allow me to bring clarity to this illustration; it is obvious that the first two people that we were first introduced to were JoJo and Vanessa. We then see that they are on opposite sides on the gym holding a rope/cord, which symbolized a physical separation. It is important to notice that even though these two were separated physically, we see the six people that enter into the gym and walk into the middle and grab hold of the knot that is in the middle of the rope/cord. These six people symbolize three of JoJo's demons that he was dealing with and the other three symbolized Vanessa's, and the knot symbolized their spiritual soul tie.

Now it is important to notice that no matter how far and long these two separate from each other, they cannot separate that easily. The six people that entered into the gym, which symbolized each of their demons- three from Vanessa end and three from JoJo's end- remained in the middle and connected themselves unto the knot, which symbolized the soul tie that was created between JoJo and Vanessa when they first had sex. This means that the soul ties were not broken. As you can see, soul ties do have nothing to do with the physical, but it has everything to do with unclean spirits coming together and keeping a people bound spiritually.

    I pointed out these key and important factors regarding sex and soul ties because when a person is molested or raped, even though they don't willingly commit to have sex with their molester or rapist, the fact that the man came into the woman immediately, a soul tie was created. Bringing it close to home, you may see young women or men at an early age that is very promiscuous; it is very possible that if that young woman or man was fondled with as a child, the spirit of the molester or rapist has connected and became one with that child spirit being, meaning that child has been contaminated, and their innocence and identity has been stripped from them. For some of you parents who are aware that your child was messed with, you have seen the change in your child's behavior. The change doesn't always happen over night; for some people, it happens over years, and for others, it's more instant.

    Soul ties are real and serious. One of the fastest ways for a spirit to attach itself to an individual is by two people having sex. Once again, when two people have sex, their spirit men becomes one and a spiritual soul tie is created. Many young people are walking around with sexual desires at a young age and they can't explain nor control their sexual tendencies that they are feeling, and for some of these young people, it is because of the soul tie or the spirit of the molester or rapist that connected itself to the child. If this is not dealt with correctly from the beginning, that spirit will lie dormant for years until one gets older, then the spirit manifest itself through many ways; some ways:

1. The person might go through a time of deep depression
2. The person might go through times of self-rejection and sometimes it can turn into self-hate.
3. The person might go through thoughts of suicide. Feelings and thoughts of not wanting to live anymore.
4. The person might feel like he or she is the only person that has been through what they been through and no one will understand them, self-deception.
5. They will have thoughts of feeling like it's their fault so they go through a time of blaming themselves.
6. They might go

HERSTORY BREAKING THROUGH DARKNESS

through a time of feeling ashamed of what happened to them.

7. It is possible that they will eventually go through a rebellious stage
8. Some turn to drugs and alcohol
9. For some, their friends will change; they might start hanging with a rebellious people
10. Their attitude will change tremendous. He or she might be, at one point of time, a happy child, and eventually they go from being happy, energetic and out-going to always being irritable, isolated and sad.
11. They will either become sexually active early or become promiscuous very early one
12. This is for some, not all; they will go through a stage of confusion of sexual preference. It is possible that they will go through mental battles with their sexual identity in the sense of feeling like they were actually suppose to be born the opposite

gender. Or simply, they will be attracted to same sex gender.

13. Once again, some fall into a state of depression and might never come out of it. These people might be really quiet and isolated. They are the people who are sometimes identified as "emo." These are the people that is over looked or considered weird or unpopular. They typically deal with their problems internal instead of externally like others.

14. They deal with deep feelings of insecurity

15. They deal with low self-esteem and, once again self-rejection and self-harm

16. Self- harm can fall in many categories; it varies from cutting, over indulgence in sex, smoking, drinking, other drugs, eating disorders such as bulimia, binge eating, etc.

Those were just a list of some things. I'm pretty sure the list can be

HERSTORY BREAKING THROUGH DARKNESS

longer, but I wanted to give a general understanding that can help parents and people in general identify behaviors in their child (ren) who might have been fondled with. I believe it is very important for people to understand that when one is taken advantage of sexually, whether as a child or older, their molester takes a part of the individual with them. As I have stated before, a part of that person's identity is taken from them, especially a child.

As a child, one's identity and innocence is taken from them, and as they get older, they go through many different changes rather it be dress style, hair style, change of names, sexual preferences, etc., that person is actually on a search of trying to find him or her self-their identity.

I know some of you are thinking how do you deal with this thing either for yourself or for your child. The first thing will be to admit what have happened to you

MERCEDES JOHNSON

and to tell the whole story. Like I stated in the beginning for some of us, we partially tell what happened to us because we are afraid of what people will say and getting judged from people. But let me tell you that have been a trick of the devil to try to keep your mouth shut to never expose the situation. The devil know that you will never be fully free if you never tell the whole story; he need to be exposed. So the first thing you must do for your freedom is tell the whole truth; either talk to someone you are close to or write it out. No matter how much you cry and how bad it may hurt, let it go by exposing it completely.

Second, you have to come to place in your heart of forgiving the individual including yourself. I have learned through experience that it is easy for one to forgive the individual, but it's harder to forgive self. It is important that you go through forgiveness not simply for the person, but for yourself. If you do not forgive the person and yourself, unforgiveness will seep in your heart, and when unforgiveness comes in, it opens the door for bitterness and hatred. Forgiveness has to take its course. And lastly, I believe this part can take the longest, it can be the hardest, but it's the most important part, and it is allowing the Lord to heal you. This part can be the longest process because for many people who have been molested, especially at a young age, they go through a stage of being angry, then eventually it turns into being numb. They go numb by drinking, using street drugs, or indulging in sexual activities, and by doing these things, they become numb to the pain to the point some people tend to forget about the situation as a whole. These people appear to be mean, hard, cold and emotionless. Once again, this part can be the longest process because in order to get to the root of the problem, you have to deal with the layers on top of it.

MERCEDES JOHNSON

During this process, the person have to be willing to go through it. It's not easy. It will hurt. To bring it to a practical sense, think of a person who always workout but never go to a masseuse, and when they finally go see one, the masseuse mentions that the individual have numerous knots throughout their body. They tell the individual it's going to be a process, meaning they are going to have several sessions in order to get all the knots out. During the sessions, the masseuse gives the individual a towel and instruct him/her to take his or her clothes off. After that step, he or she is instructed to lie flat on his or her stomach on the chaise lounge. The masseuse begins to talk while they figure out which part of the body they are going to start on first. When they begin to knead out the built-up fluid, it can be the worst feeling ever, and one's body immediately tenses up and the individual makes groaning sounds or even scream.

HERSTORY BREAKING THROUGH DARKNESS

This example is no different from one going through the process of healing. It's not a one-time thing and you're done. No! Sometimes, it can take months and even years. It's a process. It will take you back to some incidents that you have forgotten about, but the reason why you must go back to those places is because you still need to be healed in those areas. Another reason is because you have to experience that pain, you have to feel it so that you can understand for yourself that you need to be healed from it. We cannot know we need to be healed from something if we never allow ourselves to feel the pain.

When I went through my healing for this specific thing, it took me years. There were days when I thought that I was okay and I free, and there were days when I hated him and myself. My emotions were unstable, so through my healing process, my mind and emotions needed to be free and healed from the trauma that it

MERCEDES JOHNSON

caused. God doesn't heal partially, but completely.

Lets pray. Father, we bless you and we thank you in advance for your healing power in Jesus name. We thank you for deliverance that has been taking place in the minds of your children. We thank you for already beginning the process, Lord. In the power of the Holy Ghost, I break and sever all emotional, spiritual and sexual soul ties now in the mighty name of Jesus. I break it now! I set fire upon every ungodly soul tie in the name of Jesus. I bind up the plot and plan of the enemy in the lives, mind, soul (will, mind and emotions), home, and body in the name of Jesus. Every area that the enemy has a foothold in, I expose it now in the mighty name of Jesus. I expose the plans of the enemy in your life and your family life. I bind that spirit of mental manipulation that have you thinking that everything that happened to you is your fault. I bind that lying spirit now in the name of Jesus. I pull down the lies and strongholds in your mind now! I expose

HERSTORY BREAKING THROUGH DARKNESS

every lie by the word of God. I bind that spirit of seduction now in the name of Jesus. I call it forth now. I call it from your mind. I call it from your spirit. I call it from your emotions now in the mighty name of Jesus. I declare, it cannot and will not stay any longer. I expose it. I uncover it now in the name of Jesus. Wherever it lies dormant, I expose it. I send the fire of the Holy Ghost upon it now. I scatter every seducing spirit, every lustful demon, every compromising demon, every manipulating demon, every serpent spirit I call you out now in the mighty name of Jesus. I take authority over your plots, schemes, tactics and plans in the name of Jesus. I strip you of your power now. I apply the blood of Jesus against you in the name of Jesus. I cause you to come out the child's mind now in the mighty name of Jesus. I bind up sexual pictures, thoughts and visions now in the mind. I apply the blood of Jesus over your eyes, your mind, your eyes and your spiritual gates and doors. I apply the blood of Jesus. I loose freedom over

MERCEDES JOHNSON

your spirit now in the mighty name of Jesus. I loose liberty over your mind. and your soul in the name of Jesus. I declare your freedom in the name of Jesus. I decree that from this day forward, the chains are broken off you. The chains are broken off your mind, your heart, your spirit and your soul. I prophesy your freedom in the mighty name of Jesus. I prophesy from this day forth that you will walk into your freedom and your destiny in the name of Jesus. I prophesy that the little girl that carried insecurities, depression, low self-esteem and rejection is now being broken from that place today. I declare that from this day forward, you are going to walk in total victory and deliverance. The things that use to bother you, hurt you, and torture you will no longer affect you. I prophesy that you are walking into your victory and your freedom. I see you coming forth from your grave and that place call death. You were once in a spiritual death, and everything around you was dying, but I see

HERSTORY BREAKING THROUGH DARKNESS

life coming to you. I see you coming out of the place of death and coming out your grave. I speak life into your soul, your heart, mind, body, lungs, liver, muscular system, skeletal system, circular system and your nervous system. I speak healing, deliverance, freedom and life over you in the name of Jesus. I decree that from this day forth, the fruit of the spirit (love, joy, peace, long suffering, goodness, gentleness, faith, and self-control) will fill every area in your temple in Jesus name. Amen.

MERCEDES JOHNSON

THE UNFORGETTABLE

HERSTORY BREAKING THROUGH DARKNESS

1
The Unforgettable
~ ~ ~ ~

HAVE YOU EVER witnessed something that you never saw coming? I mean, something that you never thought would happen to you? Such an experience that caused your stomach to turn rapidly, beads of sweat form on your forehead, and saliva fills the inside of your mouth. It's this experience that continues to play in your head day after day. It is this experience that will cause one to lose their mind. This is what I call the unforgettable. It is this experience that would break you, shake you, or make you. It is this experience that can overtake the mind and cause one to live in a place of depression. It is this experience that causes one to continue to live and stay in the place of when the experience first took place. This is the experience that will paralyze an individual mentally, physically and spiritually.

How does one recover from such a trauma? How should one recover? Where are the experts to coach one through this trauma? Where were the signs and warnings? Where were you, God? Where were you?

It is in the midst of this experience that makes one question the existence of God. It makes you wonder why would God allow such a thing to happen. Why didn't he protect you? Why didn't he prevent it from happening? This experience penetrates the mind in a fatal position, that of a fetus position and bombards it with questions of, "Why, God?" It is from this traumatic position in life that an individual walk through the storms of life wandering aimlessly with no direction and guidance from the Lord because they have subconsciously shut out the existence of God.

It is these experiences that leads individuals to the overindulgence of drugs

HERSTORY BREAKING THROUGH DARKNESS

and alcohol, which leads to an addiction. It is these experiences that usually happen in our childhood that affects us in our adult life. For some of us, by the time we enter into our adulthood, we are emotionally unstable, financially unstable, and have some form of addiction whether it be alcohol, chemical dependency, eating disorder (obesity or anorexia), poverty mentality (never having money or always spending money to feel good about yourself), and the list goes on.

One main effect, I believe, these traumatic experiences attack is the mind of the individual. Before I go any further, I have a question for you all, have you ever tried to hold a conversation with another adult and in the midst of you all's conversation, you realize either in the beginning or toward the middle that the person's intellect, comprehension, and vocabulary is at the level of a child's? I'm sure many of you have come across someone like this, and the first thing that came to mind is that something is definitely wrong with the individual, which to some degree is correct, but the labels we place on them isn't always correct.

The reason I'm taking time to highlight this situation is because there are many people in the world including some of you who are reading this book that have created a habit in your life due to a trauma in your childhood, and this habit have followed you now into your adulthood. No, all habits is not bad, there are good ones, but I am talking those habits that have become apart of your personality, your mentality and your subconsciousness. These are the habits that have slipped into your subconsciousness without your consent. You all know our ways when we say, "Well, this is how I am and this is how I have always been." However, this may have been how you have conducted yourself for as long as you have known, but it does not mean that it is good for you.

All of us have

HERSTORY BREAKING THROUGH DARKNESS

experienced or even witnessed traumas in our childhood or for some of you, even now in your adulthood that have paralyzed you in every way possible, and the way you perceive certain things and people are formed based off your trauma. You live with this traumatic experience daily, and you refuse to let people in, you refuse to admit to people that you are still traumatized by what your father did to you when you was a little girl or a little boy, you refuse to admit that you are still traumatized by seeing your mother constantly beat your younger siblings day and night. You are still traumatized, but you refuse to admit it, you refuse to acknowledge the deep scars and wounds.

Not too long ago, I was watching a movie called *Don't Say a Word*, staring with Michael Douglas and Brittany Murphy. Brittany Murphy plays a trouble young girl who witnessed her father killed by a gang of men. Ten years after the murder of her father, teenage Elisabeth (Brittany Murphy) has been sentenced to a mental institute and haven't spoken about the murder scene since the time it happened.

Throughout the movie, psychiatrist, Dr. Nathan, (Michael Douglas) works with young Elisabeth to get some numbers from her that she has held deep in her since the killing of her father, and it is these numbers that she have that the gang that killed her father is still in need of.

What was intriguing about the movie is the fact that during Elisabeth's time of being in the mental institute, she began to take on the personalities and behaviors of other patients around her and mastered them. Why would she do that? Great question, she was afraid and didn't want to face what was outside of the four walls.

She witnessed her father beat and killed at a young age by a gang of men, and not only that she had something that she knew they wanted, and she was aware that they were still out looking for her. This young girl went out her way to avoid it, so she

HERSTORY BREAKING THROUGH DARKNESS

stayed locked up in mental institutes because of the trauma that she witnessed, and it paralyzed and injected her with fear. Some of the psychiatrists did not bother to look at the root of Elisabeth's file; they ignored the fact that this teenage girl was relocated to numerous mental institutions. When Dr. Nathan, (Michael Douglas) began working with her, he led her to the root of the problem. He asked her questions that made her squirm and cry, but it was the first time in ten years of her speaking about the murdering of her father as well as admitting that she was scared.

I know some of you are thinking to yourself like what does this have to do with anything? It has a lot to do with a lot. There's so many of us who has allowed our past experiences and traumas to paralyze us. We have allowed fear to grip us, and the job of fear is to keep us locked in and never move forward from that place. Some of you have nice careers, degrees and families, which is great but still with all that you have accomplished, fear still have a lock

MERCEDES JOHNSON

on you. You have accomplished so much in life to prove to others that you are not what they said you would be. All of your accomplishments are to prove someone or yourself wrong. It is all a mask. Underneath the make-up, underneath the mask, you are wounded, hurt and broken. You have not let go. The imagines have not left your mind so you smoke and drink to numb the hurt and wash away the vivid images. It's hard for you to remain sober for a day because you don't want to be reminded. You don't want to be reminded that even though you have made it out of the hood, you have invested in your own business and established your family, you are still broken, and the only way that you are going to be able to break free is admitting to yourself that are not okay, you are not that person that you have made people to believe that you are. You have to be real with yourself in order to help and free yourself.

Before I proceed, there is someone who is reading this and immediately you

HERSTORY BREAKING THROUGH DARKNESS

began to think about how people will respond to you if they knew the real you, and instantly, your mind was full with the thoughts of being in a weakened position. Growing up, you were considered the weak one because you always displayed your feelings and emotions, and instead of people taking them into consideration, you were talked about and walked over. As time went by and you got older, you developed an outer shell of hardness, and you covered up who you really are. People around you consider you to be the hard one out the group; you don't take mess from no one around you. For so long, you have lived behind this mask, built up hurt, pain, and anger. Deep down, you hate the person that you have become. You feel like you can't let people in. You feel like you can't be real with people because for so long you have lived behind a mask and a wall to the point that you don't even know where and how to start to be real. A part of you refuse to go back to the vulnerable and weak person that you use to be, and you

MERCEDES JOHNSON

made a promise to yourself by any means necessary you will never allow another person to see you weak.

The way you feel is real and very understandable, but I will say that crying does not mean that you are weak neither does being vulnerable; it does mean that you are just as human as everybody else. I want to tell you that you don't have to continue to carry this weight and burden on your own any more. You can release it. This burden that has been weighing you down; do not have to be a part of your future if you do not want it to be. You don't have to live your life behind a mask any longer; you can snatch it off and come from behind it. You can do it. It doesn't matter what people have to say. You don't have to live your life under the circumstances of others and wondering what they think about you. You can free yourself from pleasing people and trying to prove them wrong. You have tricked yourself for so long into thinking that you don't care about what people think about

HERSTORY BREAKING THROUGH DARKNESS

you, but what you have failed to realize is that half of your life has been about proving your worth to those around you. Today, you can come from under their supervision. Today, you can actually live for yourself. Today, you can actually breathe. Today, you can have the choice to confront the mask you been living behind for years. Today, you can snatch your identity back by acknowledging the mask you been living with. No one is going to judge you. No one is going to look at you as weak. What's more important is your sanity, your freedom and your mind. Free yourself not for me, but for you and begin to be honest and real with yourself. I believe in you. I charge you woman; I charge you man to confront the mask of pretend, self-deception, self-manipulation, self-rejection, pride, hurt, jealousy, and envy; look that thing in the face that has stolen your identity for years of your life and reclaim your life, freedom and identity. Tell that thing that you will no longer allow it to rule over your life, but from this day forward, you will be real to yourself and with yourself in Jesus name. Amen.

2
The Reality Of The Unforgettable
~ ~ ~ ~

I WALKED AROUND in our small apartment moping while I watched Mama get dressed in her room. As I was watching her, Mama turned around and faced me with a huge smile on her face, "Jada," she said with her smile plastered on her face. "I told you when I get back, we are still going to make nachos and watch movies, I promise."

I looked at Mama with tears in my eyes, "I don't want you to leave. You promised we were going to make nachos and watch movies. I don't want you to go."

"Jada, I told you I'm coming back."

"But I don't want you to go," I said, following

MERCEDES JOHNSON

Mama throughout the apartment with tears staining my face.

I didn't want Mama to leave. A couple of days ago, Mama and I decided that we would spend some time together, just her and I. My mind was set on us spending time together. These were the moments I enjoyed more than anything. There were no interruptions, distractions, and most importantly Mama gave me her undivided attention.

As I watched mama get dressed, Le-Le, Mama's friend's daughter came in the apartment greeting Mama and I with a loud voice.

"Hey, Le-Le," Mama and I said in unison.

I watched her as she took her jacket and shoes off swiftly in the living room. Eventually, my attention was turned back to Mama who was looking at me with a smirk on her face. I knew she thought with Le-Le being at the house with me, my

HERSTORY BREAKING THROUGH DARKNESS

attention would've been focused on Le-Le, but on this particular day that wasn't the case. I couldn't focus on anything else except the fact how she was leaving, and I didn't want her to go. This day was different from any other day, and I couldn't shake the feeling I felt about Mama leaving. I'm sure she got use to me hounding her about her whereabouts and my ranting and crying when she left, but this day, I couldn't shake.

"Mom, I don't want you to go. You said you were going to stay in with me. I don't want you to go." Tears welled and fell from my eyes down my cheeks as I continually repeated the promise Mama made to me as if she had amnesia.

"I know what I said, Jada, and we are still going to cook nachos and watch movies, look," Mama said while pointing in the direction of the kitchen counter where the nacho cheese and meat were located. I guess that was Mama's way of indicating to me that she didn't forget

MERCEDES JOHNSON

about the plans that we had made a couple of days ago.

"You promise?"

"I promise."

"Promise?" I yelled one last time as Mama was heading out the door.

As Mama was getting ready to close the heavy door behind her, she turned around looking in my direction with her million-dollar smile plastered on her glowing face; her smile showed all thirty-two of her teeth. "I'll be back, baby. I promise, okay?"

My smile matched her smile as I sat on the couch looking in her direction. "Okay, Mom," I said in agreement with her.

Le-Le and I remained on the couch, watched movies, and ate candy and junk food while we waited for Mama to come back. Le-Le was like a cousin to me, and her mother was a friend of Mama's, and she was like an auntie to me. Nicole, Le-

HERSTORY BREAKING THROUGH DARKNESS

Le's mom and Mama was pretty tight; they drank and hung out together a lot. Whenever Mama and Nicole was together, they would either be at our house or over at Nicole's house. On this particular day, the party was held at Nicole house.

    I don't remember exactly what Le-Le and I were watching on television, but what I was aware of is that the clock was ticking, the night wasn't getting younger, and Mama wasn't back yet. I couldn't seem to take my mind off Mama and her promise. I was so focused on us spending time together that the thought of her not following through with her words frustrated me, and my anger began to boil on the inside of me.

    As I wrestled with my inner thoughts, frustration, and anger, I looked over at Le-Le who was slowly drifting off to sleep. Eventually, she lost the battle of trying to fight her sleep, and before I knew it, she was down for the count with her face buried under the blankets. As for me, I stayed

MERCEDES JOHNSON

awake looking at the television with my mind on Mama. I sat on the couch with hopes that she wouldn't disappoint me. I was hoping that she didn't start drinking and forgot about the promise she made to me. Sooner than later, my thoughts rocked me to sleep next to Le-Le.

I wasn't in a deep sleep when I was scared awake to banging on the front door. Both Le-Le and I jumped out of our sleep startled and shocked. Without thinking, I quickly jumped off the couch and sprinted towards the door to a frantically and panicking Nicole and her and Mama's mutual male friend Leon.

When I opened the door, Nicole's tall slim body fell into the apartment clumsily while Leon was directly behind her. I ran back over to the couch and crawled up in a bald and began to cry uncontrollable next to Le-Le, who too were screaming and crying out to her mother. As I cried, my eyes searched around aimlessly for Mama to walk through the door with her

HERSTORY BREAKING THROUGH DARKNESS

million-dollar smile flashing across her round caramel face, but she never came in.

I turned my attention back to Nicole and Leon screaming and crying out slurred words. Blood covered their shaking hands. As they screamed and cried out uncontrollably, the two of them placed their hands on the wall in hopes that the wall would stop their bodies from crashing unto the floor as their knees slowly got weaker by the seconds.

I don't know how I knew it, but as I watched Nicole and Leon cry with blood covering their hands, I knew in my heart that something was wrong with Mama. I just knew it. I knew something was wrong with her, but I didn't want to believe it. The scene was almost a blur to my nine-year old mind. I couldn't grasp what exactly what was going on. Without clear understanding but perfect knowing, I sat on the couch bewildered with tears streaming down my chubby cheeks. My mind couldn't grasp it, but my little heart knew something was wrong with Mama.

No later than thirty to forty minutes, Mama's sister came walking through the door of the apartment to the four of us, crying, and by this time, I was crying out hysterically for Mama.

"What you crying for, Jada?" my auntie asked as if she was unaware of what was going on with Mama.

I lifted my head up to her with tears still in my eyes and continually pouring down my flush face. "Mama, something is wrong with my Mama," I said, with my tears falling violently down my face.

"She'll be okay, girl. There's nothing wrong with her," she irritably said, looking at me.

My auntie, Nicole and Leon quietly talked amongst one another while I got dressed in my room to go to my auntie house.

Auntie took me to her house where my cousins, uncles and grandma were.

HERSTORY BREAKING THROUGH DARKNESS

When I walked in the apartment, I noticed how all the adults looked at me with a surprise look on their face, but no one said anything.

For the first couple of days, the adults ran around quietly back and forth from the apartment to the hospital to check up on Mama. Now I know some of you are thinking like what happened to her. Some of you have your own accusations of what might have happened to her. Can I tell you all something, just as you all are reading this in a state of confusion so was I. No one said anything to me regarding the condition of Mama. It was probably because they all were in hopes that Mama was going to get through whatever it was she was dealing with.

Okay, I'm not going to keep taking you all on this wild goose chase. The day when Mama left and went to her friend Nicole's house was the last day I saw Mama smile; the last time I heard her voice and the last time I saw her. Mama left out the house making a promise that I forced her to make to me without knowing that she wouldn't be able to keep her promise. I was left holding on to a broken promise for years of my life.

Mama had a childhood friend whom she loved dearly and this friend of hers' was my older cousin on my dad's side and her name was Raven. Raven and Mama met years before I was even thought about. The two of them met through my dad. Some of you probably know how things go when you have your boyfriend, you tend to hang with either his sister or cousin. In Mama's cases, Daddy didn't have any sisters, but he had cousins and the one she hung with was Raven.

Mama and Raven was always together; they laughed together, cried together, and more than anything, they fought each other. The two of them fought so much to the point that when the two of them were together, you can count on them fighting. They had a strange relationship that many others and myself did not understand, but I guess it worked well for the two of them. Typically, when Mama and Raven got together, there was always drinks involved, and when the two of them started drinking, they didn't stop until all the liquor and beer was gone and sometime they will go and get more. It was during these moments when Mama and Raven would fight; there was never a time when the two of them got together, and there was no liquor and fighting.

So on this particular day at Nicole's house, my cousin Raven was there as well. Nicole was having a small gathering at her house, and many other people were there at her house drinking, listening to music, and having a good time.

"Raven, go to the store and get some more beer," Mama's brother, Kevin said.

"Okay, okay, okay," Raven said in her high-pitched slur.

Uncle Kevin gave Raven the money to go to the

store to get more beer for everyone. When he gave her the money, he also told her what type of beer he specifically wanted from the store.

I don't know how Raven misinterpreted what uncle Kevin sent her to the store for, but when she came back to the apartment, she didn't have what he sent her to the store for.

"Where's my beer?" Raven wasn't all the way in the apartment when Uncle Kevin began questioning her through his slurred words.

"Dang," Raven said clearly with an attitude.

"I just got in," Raven said while taking her jacket off and walking into the living room, giving Uncle Kevin his beer that was in a brown paper bag and his change.

When Uncle Kevin looked inside the bag, he immediately noticed that Raven got the wrong type of beer.

"Raven," Uncle Kevin yelled out very boisterous.

Without waiting for

HERSTORY BREAKING THROUGH DARKNESS

her to respond, Uncle Kevin complained to her about not bringing the right beer and how he wanted her to either go back to the store to get the beer he asked her to get or give him his money back.

Mama and Uncle Kevin was really close. They were probably so close because the two of them looked alike, and many people would mistake them of being twins, and they were the only ones out of their other siblings who shared the same father.

"Raven, go back to the store and go get the right beer before I put my hands on you," Mama said boisterously, possibly because of the amount of beer and liquor she been drinking.

"I'm not going to go get nothing," Raven retorted back with the level of her voice matching Mama's. After a couple of minutes of arguing, Mama attacked her and the two of them started fighting.

Uncle Kevin and everyone else that were there

MERCEDES JOHNSON

didn't bother to stop Mama and Raven from fighting because they all were use to it. Of course, one or two of them yelled out for them to stop fighting, but when they didn't, everyone just started drinking the beer that Raven grabbed from the store.

As Mama and Raven was fighting, they started off fighting in the living room where everyone was located, and somehow as they were fighting, Mama and Raven made their way to one of the rooms in the back of the apartment. When they made their way to the book of the room, no one decided to go to the back with them because they were under the impression that the fight was going to be over, and the two of them would eventually rejoin them, but their assumptions weren't correct.

It wasn't long after Mama and Raven fighting in the back of the apartment Raven came running from the back of the apartment, and without saying a word to anyone, she made an exit out the front door. It wasn't long until Mama came from the back room and made her way to the kitchen, and when she got to the kitchen, her body collapsed to the floor. When Uncle Kevin saw his sister, his twin, hit the cold kitchen floor, he immediately jumped from off the couch and rushed over to Mama lying on the floor.

Mama had on a red shirt so Uncle Kevin and no one else in the house knew what was going on because when Raven came from the back, she ran straight out the door. As Uncle Kevin was trying to pick Mama up from off the floor, she repeatedly stated out of her mouth, "She stabbed me. She stabbed me. Raven stabbed me."

When Uncle Kevin looked down at his shirt and hands, he saw the blood and realized that Mama was bleeding and it hit him that Raven stabbed Mama while the two of them was in the back fighting. After calling the police, Uncle Kevin took off running and no one saw him the remaining of that night, and Nicole and Leon ran to

MERCEDES JOHNSON

where Le-Le and I were at while Mama was rushed to the hospital.

I know. I know. Many of you are thinking like how did Raven get the knife and where did she get it from. That is a touchy topic and question only because no one really knows where Raven got the knife. Uncle Kevin believes that my cousin Raven had the intentions of killing Mama that night, and he said that because he believed that Raven had the knife on her before they started fighting and she waited until her and mama got in the back away from everyone to stab her. However, was it intentional or not, I really don't know, but what I do know is that she pulled a knife out and stabbed Mama a couple inches away from her heart, and she was in the hospital no longer than three weeks, and she died.

Everyone around me prayed and believed that Mama was going to make it and fight through it. Everyone knew Mama to be a fighter

HERSTORY BREAKING THROUGH DARKNESS

because that's all she did was fought. All her life, she fought- physically, mentally and spiritually. In the streets of Chicago, it was rare to hear that Mama ever lost a fight. She wasn't one to mess with. I've learned by watching Mama and many others that there will be fights that we will win, and others we will lose. No matter how everyone wanted Mama to fight through, this one she didn't have the strength to fight back. Mama tried her hardest to hold on and fight the best way she knew how while in the hospital. Family and friends went to the hospital daily with balloons and cards in their hands, with tears filling and falling from the wells of their eyes.

During the couple of weeks of Mama being in the hospital, I wasn't allowed to see her so the reports that I heard about her while being in there was what I heard from friends of the family and not the family itself. I guess they thought it was better not to talk to me about it because maybe they figured I was too young or whatever the case may have been. I do know they didn't talk to me about the condition of Mama, nor was I allowed to see Mama while she was in the hospital.

As I was stating, friends of the family told me about Mama's condition in the hospital. Many said that due to the amount of alcohol that Mama consumed throughout her life that the stab wound caused her to swell up. Also, according to the doctors, it was stated that Mama had walking pneumonia. Though mama had walking pneumonia when Raven stabbed her, the stab wound was only a couple inches away from Mama's heart, meaning it was the stabbing wound that killed Mama.

While Mama was in the hospital, she was hooked up to machines, and tubes were stuck down her throat, meaning she was not able to talk. People informed me that as they would cry at the hospital, Mama would look at them shaking her head, which was her way of telling them not to cry. Others reported to me

HERSTORY BREAKING THROUGH DARKNESS

that when they went to visit Mama, she would try to talk, but the tube was stuck down her throat. Some mentioned that they actually witnessed Mama shed tears and move her head from side to side as they talked to her. The doctors instructed Mama's visitors that Mama could hear everything they said so they could talk to her, and she will hear them, but she wouldn't be able to speak back, but her body movement indicated that she heard them.

I guess it was good for many of them who were close to Mama to see her while she was in the hospital because, to their surprise, that was going to be their last time seeing her function with the little strength she was holding on to. I remember the day my auntie, granny, uncle and Mister last time coming from the hospital with tears flooding down their faces. I watched them from a distance as if I was a shadow walking among them, unbelief gripped their hearts, I remember hearing my granny say, "She was strong. She was suppose to make it through this one, but

MERCEDES JOHNSON

she let the devil win this battle." Everyone spoke around me, above me, but never to me.

During this time, my granny and my youngest uncle were on the porch, and I watched her as she told him the news that his sister was gone. I saw how his legs gave out on him, and he fell on his knees and buried his face in his hands as he cried.

"Granny, what's wrong with uncle Larry," I asked innocently, as if I didn't know what was going on.

Lifting her head up with a smile on her face she replied in a soft whisper, "Oh nothing baby, your uncle is crying because his girlfriend broke up with him," Grandma said this with a confident look on her face.

I stood there with tears in my eyes as I looked at my uncle and grandma sitting down on the ground holding one another. "It's going to be okay, Uncle," I said while placing my small red hand on his shoulder. I knew that he wasn't crying because of a girl.

HERSTORY BREAKING THROUGH DARKNESS

One thing about the streets of Chicago was that everybody talked. Word got around the streets really fast so though my family felt that it was best to keep everything from me, I heard news from people in the streets what happened with Mama and my cousin Raven.

MERCEDES JOHNSON

3
Now Behold The Unforgettable
~ ~ ~ ~

TUESDAY, JUNE 20, 2000 my auntie's house was full with bodies moving around sporadically throughout the house getting dressed for Mama's funeral. Everyone dressed in a beige/ cream-looking color. On this particular day, there wasn't a lot of laughter going on, and everyone appeared to be serious and stuck in their own zone.

I didn't say much to anyone. No one asked me how I felt about everything going on. No one yet sat down with

HERSTORY BREAKING THROUGH DARKNESS

me to tell me that this very day we all were going to Mama's funeral to say our last good-byes, though I knew what was going on, my family didn't bother to sit down with me to explain what was going on with Mama. No one bothered to tell me exactly why it has been weeks since I last seen Mama. In my nine-year-old mind and heart, I still waited for Mama to come back through the door. Even though I got word from the street about Mama and Raven, my mind couldn't grasp it because all I knew was that Mama made a promise to me, and I held on to her words. I held onto a broken promise, which caused me to shut down and push away the reality that Mama was never coming back. My mind couldn't grasp the concept that on this particular day, we were getting ready to say our last goodbyes to Mama and bury her six feet deep under dirt. I didn't believe it. One would have thought that I lived in a make- believe world. No one bothered to ask how I felt, and I didn't bother to speak about how I felt.

MERCEDES JOHNSON

We all piled up inside the limo that waited for us downstairs in the back of Robert Taylor Projects. As we all sat in the limo, we all talked among one another about the car, but never about the event that we all were dreading to face.

The all black limo pulled up to the medium-sized church house where all of Mama's friends and family stood outside waiting for us to get out of the oversized car. The people's faces seemed to be a blur to me maybe because I was trying to keep my game face on and continue to play the game of pretending that I was clueless to everything that was going on. I mastered pretending early on at an early age.

As we all made our way into the church house, people couldn't hold their tears in. Many of them began to cry before the funeral officially started. As I found the place I was going to sit, familiar faces and unfamiliar faces came up to me with tears

HERSTORY BREAKING THROUGH DARKNESS

streaking down their face, embracing my small and frail body into theirs as they repeatedly said how sorry they were. I couldn't muster up a smile, a frown or a tear. I just stood there with no expression on my face.

I found my seat and sat next to my granny who wrapped her arms around my stiff body as she sobbed on my neck. I sat and watched how the preacher got up to talk about Mama and memories that made everyone cry and other times laughed. After the preacher spoke, my auntie's children father rose up and made his way to the front. He stood there as he fought back his tears as he opened his mouth and spoke about the lasting memories him and Mama shared.

"This wonderful lady left three beautiful daughters, and her eldest Jada wrote a poem for her mother for Mother's Day, and I am going to read it," the pastor mentioned as he grabbed hold of the microphone from my auntie's children's father.

MERCEDES JOHNSON

With the mention of me, everyone looked around trying to find me amongst the many bodies throughout the funeral home. My granny must have saw or felt the tension in my body because she grabbed me and held me tighter than before.

The preacher went on to say, "Dear, Mom, I love you so much that whatever you say goes.... And roses are red, violets are blue make this love as sweet as you. I love you, Mom. You are my queen. I love you, Mom. Your daughter, Jada Rose."

Who would have known that the poem that was written for Mother's Day was going to be the same poem read one month later at your mother's funeral? Who would've thought? Who would've guessed? What do you say? What do you do? Well, I know what I did do- the best thing I was use to doing- pretend like I didn't hear it. Pretended like nothing affected me even though I was slowly breaking on the

HERSTORY BREAKING THROUGH DARKNESS

inside, but my mind wouldn't allow me to believe my reality that stood me in the face. "She promised that she will be back," was all that rang in my mind. Even though we were at Mama's funeral, I couldn't accept it, and I didn't accept it because she promised me that she would be back. She promised me that she would never leave me. She promised and I believed her.

Shortly after the reading of the poem and a song by Yolanda Adams, "Open my heart," was ministered and soon after that it was time for the last viewing of Mama. I felt the pressure in the atmosphere. This was the part where everyone dreaded. I don't think anyone wanted to face this reality, more than anything, no one wanted to face the reality that this was going to be their last time seeing Mama and actually saying good-bye, especially for those who did not plan on going to the breaking of the ground and the actual burial.

The bottom of my feet was plastered to the floor as

MERCEDES JOHNSON

my eyes was glued on the people that walked past my row as they made their way to view Mama's body. At that moment, I fought strongly with myself. Everything in me wanted to cry, but I couldn't. I couldn't allow anyone see me cry. I couldn't cry. I couldn't. Before I knew it, I felt my granny's warm hand touch my shoulder really gently, "It's our turn, baby." One would've thought that I was paralyzed from the waist down. I heard her, but I couldn't move. Maybe it was my fear and anxiety that was building up on the inside of me that finally grabbed a hold of me and paralyzed me. At the moment, I allowed myself to actually feel, and before I knew it, one tear fell from my eyes. I quickly wiped my tear away, got my game face on and walked out the row, down the aisle, and before I knew it, I stood before Mama.

    I wanted to break down and cry. I wanted to respond like everyone else, but my unbelief wouldn't allow me. *This can't be Mama.*

HERSTORY BREAKING THROUGH DARKNESS

She promised me that she would be back for me. I made her promise that she would never leave me. She promised me. She was coming back. She promised me. Mama promised me. She'll be back. This is not Mama. She promised me that she would be back.

I reached out my small shaking hand and gently touched Mama face. Just as quick as I touched her was just as quick as I pulled my hand away, and my granny placed her hand on my shoulder for a second time. I guess that was her way of letting me know that my time was over. I quietly strolled back to my seat and sat stone-faced without an ounce of emotion. I silently watched in anger while everyone hugged one another and cried.

"You are so strong," my granny said as she sat down next to me.

"Huh," I said, startled by her presence and words.

Looking at me with a smile on her face. "Everyone came up to me and mentioned how they noticed how strong you were. They mentioned how you didn't cry and how you were so strong. I told them that you are my baby, and yes, you are strong."

"Thank you, Granny," I responded with a smile plastered across my face.

As we all were getting ready to pile back in our vehicles to head to the burial site, people stopped me, giving me hugs and their condolences. I didn't know if I should have gave them hugs back because as for me and my house, Mama wasn't dead or gone, she was coming back whether they knew it or not.

4
Death, Burial, Goodbye
~ ~ ~ ~

"JADA, SAY BYE to your mom. Say bye, Jada."

I stood outside with a long stemmed red rose in my hand, watching Mama being lowered in the ground. Everyone around me repeatedly instructed me to throw the rose on Mama's casket and tell her good-bye. Quite frankly, I didn't understand what was really going on, but I did what was told of me and threw the rose on the casket, said good-bye to Mama, and I turned my around and never looked back.

I wasn't the only one that never looked back, but everyone around me. After this particular day, my family and I never sat down together and talked about the way we felt about the loosing of Mama, the day of the funeral, etc. this topic was never brought up. It almost appeared to seem that everyone pretended that it never happened. Maybe the adults felt like it would bring the pain and hurt of a reality that they never wanted to face again. What no one realized was they weren't creating an atmosphere for me as an nine-year-old child to grasp the reality of the death of her mother or the proper understanding of grieving.

The fact that no one talked to me about the death of Mama, what that did to me was furthered my own self-deception and lies of Mama coming back. It placed a muffler over my mouth,

HERSTORY BREAKING THROUGH DARKNESS

and what this muffler did was smothered me vocally to the very point that I never talked or thought about Mama after the funeral. Kids would come up to me around the projects and ask, "Hey, is your mom dead?" with an attitude, I would respond, "Is your mom dead?" by this time, I was nine years old and completely dead to my emotions and feelings. Many people around me ignorantly and blindly boosted on the strength I appeared to have, but if they only knew and saw behind my smile, innocent face and brown eyes that I was a broken, confused, hurt, and a lost little girl.

Everything I witnessed, endured and suffered, I never spoke about it. I kept it all to myself. No one knew that Mama's boyfriend was messing with me so much to the point that it messed me up mentality and brought about confusion in me regarding the understanding of love and my sexuality. This little nine-year-old girl was jacked up. My innocence and identity was snatched and taken away before I even got an understanding or acknowledgment of my identity. At the age of nine years old, I was already battling with my identity. In other words, I was having identity crises, and no one knew or paid attention.

I am stretching the fact that no one knew because it is possible that something can be happening to your child (ren) or someone else's child (ren) right before your eyes, and you or no one else pays attention to the changes in that child. Let's pay attention to our children and those around us and create a relationship and atmosphere with our child (ren) so that he or she can be comfortable enough to let you know what is going on with them. Parents do not dismiss or bypass having dialogues with your child (ren) about good and bad touch. Unfortunately, Mama and I didn't sit down to have these types of talks. Yes, a part of me was aware that something wasn't right about what Mister was doing, but when all you crave for is love and attention, as an six or seven years old, it's easy

HERSTORY BREAKING THROUGH DARKNESS

for manipulation to grip your mind and heart and pervert the true definition and understanding of true love. Don't ignore the signs.

Not only was I dealing with identity crises, but now the sudden death of Mama, the only parent that I knew and had. My biological father was still in prison, and I had no real connection with him. All I knew was Mama and right before my eyes, she too, just like my innocence, was taken from me without my consent.

Many people say they don't know how they will feel or act if they lost their parent. Even with experiencing the lost of Mama, I too will say I don't know how to act or feel about losing a parent. It's not a feeling that one can actually put in words, and for me, as I stated previously, my family and I didn't talk about it. After the funeral, it was almost like everyone went back to his or her own lives maybe because death in the projects wasn't something that was new or out the ordinary. No one came around to see

MERCEDES JOHNSON

about us during the after care. During the process of getting everything together, I saw many faces coming around to help my auntie and family, but the aftercare of the dealing and healing was never dealt with. The grieving process never took place.

Some of you are still stuck on the part that it was my cousin that killed Mama, and some of you are thinking about how did I even get through that reality. Well, to answer you all acquiring and wondering minds, um, I really don't know. It didn't register in my mind that Raven actually killed Mama. Once again, yes I was aware of her actions and that she was the cause of killing Mama, but nine years, old Raven was far from my mind more than anything the absence of Mama was more important to me.

5
Results

LOSING A PARENT of either gender is always a

MERCEDES JOHNSON

hard pill to swallow. I don't believe any one person will be able to completely get over it because it is your father or mother. In my case, it was my mother. The death of my mother hit me really hard not only because she was my mother and her death was unexpected, but also because I grew up in a single parent home so when she left, it felt like my life was taken from me. After the death of Mama, I suffered a higher level of depression, insecurity, self-rejection, self-blame, and more than anything I went through my moments of suicide thoughts and attempts.

    Listen, everyone deals with death very differently, and I don't think there is a specific way a person is to deal with it and get over it. Let's make this clear, I do not believe any person in this world will ever completely get over the death of a love one. That is not something someone can just get over. However, I do believe that there is a way one can actually deal with a death so that it don't consume and overtake the

HERSTORY BREAKING THROUGH DARKNESS

individual's mind, body and health. I also don't think that any one person can tell an individual how long it should take for them to grieve over a lost one simply because people deal with situations very differently. However, if I can suggest due to my own experience, I suggest one to not wait long to go through your grieving process. Grieving is real, and it is important.

    Another thing is if any of you are anything like me, I hated crying; I felt like it symbolized a sign of weakness, but in reality, that was another attack of the enemy that prolonged my healing process. By all means, please cry. Allow yourself to feel the pain. I meet so many people that say that the reason why they smoke or drink is because they don't want to feel certain pains of their experience, but it is better to deal with it when it is fresh than for it to catch up to you when you least expect it. One can only run for so long. You can only smoke and drink for so long until all the tactics you used run out, and the very thing that you have been trying to avoid will still be sitting there. It is better to deal with it immediately, or it will deal with you.

I know that many people look down on the idea of counseling, but when one is dealing with something this critical, counseling will be good. Single mothers or fathers, if your child have experienced the lost of one of their parents please put that child in counseling early on. Do not wait until they get older because sometimes, by the time they get older, they probably have found other alternatives to deal with it, which might not be the best way to deal with it.

As for me, it took me years of dealing with the death of Mama because it took me years to first accept the fact that she was actually dead and wasn't coming back. As crazy as that might sound, but I was so engulfed in my own self-deception that I never really acknowledged it enough to myself to actually break that strong hold/ lie that had captured my mind and held me in bondage mentally for years. So once again, the first step for me to allow grieving and healing to take place was confronting that lie and pull down that stronghold. To be honest, it took someone from the outside to look me in the face and repeatedly yell "Your mom is gone, she is dead, and isn't coming back. Now cry, let it go and cry." This was the first step of my on-going process of healing.

Second, I had to acknowledge the inner anger I had towards Mama. I know. I know. How did I hold anger towards a dead person? But it is true I was angry and fierce toward Mama, and that was one of my reasons of never talking about her because my deep bitterness that was slowly forming hatred toward Mama.

The anger and bitterness formed in my heart toward Mama due to another level of self-deception, which was the broken promise that I forced Mama to make to me. When she didn't fulfill her promise, it opened the door for disappointment to come in, which eventually turned into anger and bitterness. So once again, I walked around for years unaware of this hurt, anger, disappointment, and bitterness in my heart simply because I mentally and emotionally closed that chapter of my life and never had any intentions of revisiting it.

Once again, someone from the outside walked up to me and boldly told me that I needed to let go of something that I have been holding on. At first, I to went back and forth with the young lady stating that I wasn't holding on to anything and how I was doing fine in my life, oh how wrong was I.

That night, when I got home, I sat in my bedroom pondering on the statement the lady made, and for the first time, I traveled back to the day when Mama walked out the door and never came back and immediately tears filled the wells of my eyes. My body instantly tensed up and anger took over me. At that moment for the first time, I vocally voiced how I felt about the

HERSTORY BREAKING THROUGH DARKNESS

death of Mama and how it made me feel. For the first time, I didn't pretend like I had it altogether, I cried, yelled and cuss words came forth like vomit.

At that very moment, it was evident that I had stored up hurt that eventually turned into anger and bitterness. I couldn't understand for the life of me why Mama had to leave. I felt lied to and betrayed. I felt like she left me. She left me alone in this world, and I couldn't understand. For the first time, I confronted my hurt, anger, bitterness, and most importantly, the unforgiveness that I allowed to harbor in my heart.

Many of you are thinking where and how did the unforgiveness come in. The unforgiveness came in when Mama didn't come back that night. I made her promise to me that she will be back. I made her promise, and I counted on her to come back, and when she didn't, it was hard for me to accept the understanding and the reality that Mama was killed. In my head, I looked at it as her leaving me.

MERCEDES JOHNSON

Disappointment eventually sat in my heart, and over time, unforgiveness came in and took over. I realized at that moment that I loved Mama so much, and in the same breath, I hated her the more for leaving me. I didn't want her to leave, and everything in me wanted her to come back, but no matter how much I wish she were still here, I accepted the truth that Mama was dead. She didn't deliberately leave me. She was killed and more than anything Mama loved me just as much as I loved her, and if it were up to her, she would've stayed with me.

This wasn't the first and last time I had to confront this particular thing, it took days, weeks, months, even years of constant admitting and crying. My healing and deliverance took as long as it did for me because of the layers and years of pretending and living behind a mask.

The last step for my healing was taking time to journal and cry. For so long, I lived the lie of thinking that crying was a sign of weakness. Throughout the years, I practiced controlling my emotions until I began a professional. There were times when I will want to cry, but the tears wouldn't come out.

What helped me to release my bottled up emotions was journaling. Writing became my getaway of the real world. The ink from the pen took place of my heart and feelings that was placed on the papers in my journals. Following the ink was my emotions that were integrated with fearless tears. My journal became my new best friend, and my tears became apart of me that I once hated, but soon began to embrace and appreciate. I learned to deal with a lot of my unsettled emotions and feelings through an ink pen and a bounded journal.

From then to now, journaling is still my getaway to release my bottled-up emotions. It is when I am alone with my pen and journal where I find a sense of freedom and peace.

Let me tell someone who is reading this, listen,

MERCEDES JOHNSON

healing is a process, and within every phase or stage of life, you will always find yourself needing a part of your soul, (mind, will and emotions) healed. Healing is a beautiful thing that you should never neglect or regret. Remember, that everyone's healing process is different, which means what might have worked for me might not work for the next person. I highly suggest that you find something that you enjoy, whether it be walking in a park, sitting by water, going to a cabin, etc., whatever brings you peace and a sense of freedom where you can express your bottled up emotions and pain. Make sure to find a place where you don't have to be afraid of crying and being your authentic self.

Remember, we are triune beings, meaning we are made of three components: body (flesh), soul (will, mind, emotions) and spirit. The many things that we experience in life are locked up in our soul, and though some of us might go to church and have

HERSTORY BREAKING THROUGH DARKNESS

received the spirit of God, which is good, but the Holy Spirit only dwell in the component of our spirit and not our soul. What does this mean? It means that our soul man, (will, mind, emotions) still need to be healed and delivered. The hurt, anger, jealousy, perversion, bitterness, unforgiveness, etc., still lie dormant in our soul, and until we acknowledge and confront it, they will remain hidden within our soul, and we will never experience the peace and freedom that many of us yearn for. It's not enough to have an amazing career, husband and family, but still a slave to things that have happened to us years ago. It is not worth it. It is not worth living behind a mask and pretending to be happy when in reality you are miserable, depressed, fearful, angry, bitter, etc., and you know what? The only person that can change it is you. No amount of money in the world will ever be able to bring you peace and freedom. Your own family will not be able to do so because you are afraid to confront yourself. You are afraid to confront the lie you been living with for half of your life. Many of you feel like you don't even know the person you have become. You hate looking in the mirror. You question yourself, "Who is this person I have become?" But let me tell you, you have allowed the hurt, bitterness, depression, unforgiveness and rejection from your past to control your life, and it have snatched away your true identity and have given you their mask of identity. Bottom line is this, you are in bondage, and until you are ready to confront yourself, you will forever remain in bondage. You need to be delivered and healed.

CONCLUDE

Conclusion

HerStory Breaking Through Darkness is the journey of nine-year-old Jada Rose who endured almost every test and trail that should've, would've and could've killed her or paralyzed her from ever being all that God have called her to be.

I want to prophesy to all of you who are reading this book, and you who have experienced any of the things that this young lady has been through. Before I release the

HERSTORY BREAKING THROUGH DARKNESS

Word of God, I want to explain to you all the reason why I only expressed the events Jada went through from the ages four to nine. It is because it was these events that I call seeds, and these seeds were planted inside her soul, (will, mind, emotions). In this context the soul is looked upon as a garden. Inside of this young girl's garden/ soul, (will, mind, emotions) was the seeds of rejection, hatred, hurt, depression, anger, neglect, self-rejection, sexual abuse, perversion, manipulation, intimidation, confusion, bitterness, poverty, misunderstanding, etc. This is important to know because the destruction and attack on Jada's life did not start when she got older, but it was from her childhood.

Seeds can only remain hidden for so long, but eventually, these seeds will spring forth into its full effect. Some seeds will birth later or sooner than others, but what remains the same is that these seeds will come forth eventually.

MERCEDES JOHNSON

It is important to understand that seeds can be planted by way of conversation, environment, relationships, generational, sexual, psychological, and emotional and lastly, the way we respond to people, situations, changes, and conversations. These seeds have the potential to destroy your present and your future. So if we are not careful or lack the understanding or clarification of the different type of seeds that have been planted in our garden/soul (especially when we are younger), these seeds will mold and form our being, our character, the way we think, our emotions, and our appetite, meaning the things that are appealing to us. If these seeds are never acknowledged and plucked out of your garden/soul, they will grow, and before we know it, we will find ourselves having trust issues, bad anxiety, separation anxiety, low self-esteem, addictions to porn, addictions to sex, addiction to drugs, bad anger issues, unforgiveness and the list can go on and on.

HERSTORY BREAKING THROUGH DARKNESS

The results and manifestations of these seeds that were planted in our childhood and without proper dealings with these internal problems, which express their self externally can lead a person on the path of mental depression, suicidal attempts, drug habits, mental illness, etc. It is important to deal with the root of every external behavior because behind every behavioral expression, there is an internal root, which is connected to the seed that was planted in the garden/soul of the individual from their childhood.

MERCEDES JOHNSON

Prayer / Prophetic Word / Release
~ ~ ~ ~

I THANK ALL of you who have joined me on and through the journey of nine-year-old Jada Rose's story of breaking through darkness. Once again, the underlining message and purpose of this book, *HerStory Breaking Through Darkness,* was to peel back the blinders off of many of your eyes and to be bring recognition, clarity and light to the corruptible seeds that we have within us and our children. Also, so we can be aware of the seeds we have planted in our children by the way we talk to them, not spending time with them or affirming them with words of affirmation. These types of behaviors sow seeds of rejection, and rejection is one of the leading forces that have positioned itself in almost every person garden/soul. I pray that this book, especially after journeying with Jada, heightened your discernment, and revelation and that knowledge was released in you as well as things being unlocked. More than anything, I pray that this book has brought to your soul, (mind, will, emotions) complete healing and deliverance and that you will no longer be afraid to confront yourself and deal with yourself. Break yourself and your family free from generational curses and internal bondages.

MERCEDES JOHNSON

RELEASE
~ ~ ~ ~

I PROPHESY OVER every one of you who has stood in the gap for yourself, and your family as you journeyed with me throughout these pages. The chains that once held you in bondage are now falling off of you. The chains that bound your mind, spirit, soul (will, mind, emotions) are now falling off now in the mighty name of Jesus. I prophesy to the winds of healing and prosperity to meet you where you are now physically, spiritually and mentally. The winds of

HERSTORY BREAKING THROUGH DARKNESS

healing and prosperity will fill you up and overtake you. I declare that the chains of poverty are broken off of you now in the name of Jesus. I declare that the chains of addiction be broken off of you now in the mighty name of Jesus. I call the chemicals in your brain to come together in alliance, wherever there has been chemical imbalance, I call it to come into balance now in the mighty name of Jesus. I free your mind from the very desire of smoking and drinking in the name of Jesus. I bind that spirit of dependency now in the mighty name of Jesus. I break the need of chemical dependency to feel free from your pain and childhood. I break it now in the mighty name of Jesus. I bind up that strongman of addiction now in the mighty name of Jesus. There's someone in particular that is reading this, and as you are reading this, tears are flooding down your face. You come from a family of drug addiction, and there have been times when you have tried many times to stop smoking, but you found yourself going back to it. You

MERCEDES JOHNSON

have told your friends and family that you were going to stop, and everybody laughed at you and took it as a joke because they didn't believe you. They didn't think that you could stop. But I want to tell you as I am writing this, I hear the spirit of the Lord saying today you are free from that demon of addiction that have been trying to sabotage and destroy your life since your teenage years. You first started smoking at the age of twelve, and it got worst by the time you turned fourteen, right before your fifteenth birthday. I hear the spirit of the Lord saying that He is going to use you to break this generational spirit of addiction off your family. I hear the spirit of the Lord saying on this day He is freeing your spirit and mind from this addiction. The Lord said the same people that have talked about you and looked down on you are going to come to you and ask you how were you able to kick that habit. The Lord said you would glorify His name and point people into His direction in the name of Jesus. Amen.

HERSTORY BREAKING THROUGH DARKNESS

I speak blessings over all of you in the name of Jesus. I pray that God be a fence around you and your family now in the name of Jesus. Let the power of the Holy Ghost keep you in this season, time, and year during this time of life. There is someone who is reading this, and you have been going through a lot of attacks, and the attacks are particular in the area of your marriage. For the past couple of weeks, you and your spouse have been talking about getting a divorce. Your marriage has been under attack for months now. The attack actually started a year ago, but for some reason, it feels like within the last couple of months, the attacks have increased and have gotten to the point where you two are considering divorce. But I hear the Spirit of the Lord saying guess again, go back again and get it right. The Lord said the minute you two follow through with your divorce, you will experience more hell than you are having now. I hear the Spirit of the Lord say that He has put this marriage together, and the fact that He is trying to use you all's marriage as a godly marriage before family members and peers, that is why the attack has been coming the way they have. There's a ministry within you all's marriage, and if you two hold on to the promise of God, He will surely bring you two through. Amen. Lastly, wife and husband, forgive one another and allow God to heal the emotional wounds that were caused throughout the early years of your marriage through infidelity, lies, and secrets being kept from another one. Hold on to the promise of God, and He will surely bring you two through this storm and fire. Amen.

I pray that the spirit of the Lord be upon you all and your family from this generation and the generations to come. I call forth purity over your minds, the members of your body, your spirit, your relationships, your communication skills, your soul, and your heart. I release purity over you. Wherever there is corruption, I call forth cleanliness and purity in the mighty name of Jesus. I decree that you shall be free from impurity in your life; I bind the sexual images and thoughts that clutter your mind and thoughts now in the mighty name of Jesus. I cover your eye gates in the name of Jesus. I seduce proof your mind in the name of Jesus. I seduce proof your conversations in the name of Jesus. I seduce proof your environment in the mighty name of Jesus. I seduce proof your family linage and your blood stream in the mighty name of Jesus. I release the spirit of purity over you now in the mighty name of Jesus. Amen.

    I call your life to come into alignment and plans that God has for your life. I remove every distraction in your life rather it be relationally, emotionally and mentally. I remove these distractions now in the name of Jesus. I remove the blinders that has been on your eyes that have blinded you from seeing those around you who are and isn't for you. I decree prophetic alignment in your life. I call forth the success and potential that you have stored up

MERCEDES JOHNSON

on the inside of you. I awaken your potential. I awaken your dreams. I awaken your gifts. I awaken you from the place of slumber. I bind that spirit of slothfulness now in the name of Jesus. I break it off your mind now. I declare that slothfulness and laziness will no longer hover over you and control your energy, motivation, and emotions. I break it now in the name of Jesus. I release your spirit from the bondage of poverty now. I strip it off your mind. I strip it off your emotions. I strip it out of your DNA now in the mighty name of Jesus. I prophesy the spirit of freedom is hitting you right now in the mighty name of Jesus. You shall be able to live again. You shall be able to dream again. You shall be able to breathe again. I want to tell someone who is reading this everything that was stolen and taken from you in this year alone you will get it back double fold. I hear the Spirit of the Lord telling me to tell you that He haven't forgotten about, you and I prophesy to you as the Spirit of the

HERSTORY BREAKING THROUGH DARKNESS

Lord leads me, that by the end of this month, you shall see doors opening and things turning around in your favor. I hear the Spirit of the Lord say your big return is going to start in this month. I don't know exactly what it is, but you have been waiting on something from the government, and at one point, you said just forget about it, but the Lord said your big return is getting ready to come in Jesus name. Amen

I release the Glory of God over you all and your children in the name of Jesus. I break every generational curse off your family in the name of Jesus. I prophesy that it stop with you, and it will not even come near your children in the name of Jesus. I reach in the spirit of God and wipe your children sleight clean in the name of Jesus. I release a spirit of excellence over your sons and daughters now in the name of Jesus. I release abundance of knowledge and wisdom into the right and left side of their brain. I prophesy that they will not fit in the category that society and statistics has set for them, but they will live above the statistics in the name of Jesus. I release education into their future in the name of Jesus. I bind the spirit of failure, not good enough, self- rejection, intimidation, low self-esteem, insecurities, pride and arrogance. I decree that your children will not follow the in crowds or compromise their identity or standards to fit in with the "popular" group. I prophesy by the power of God that they shall be leaders, world changers, kingdom shakers, and lawmakers in the name of Jesus. They shall seek the will of God and sit under the counsel of the Lord. They shall lie before the altar of the Lord like the days of Samuel in the mighty name of Jesus. Amen.

There is someone, actually a handful of you, who have small children ranging from the ages of thirteen months and six years old, and your children have been getting attacked in their sleep nonstop. It have gotten to point where you as the parent are scared for your child and you don't know what to do because the things that your child has been describing you cannot comprehend with your physical mind. One of you in particular can sense that there's a prophetic mantle on your son's life, and actually, before you were pregnant with your son, a Prophet prophesied to you the birth of your son. This prophet of God identified to you the gender of the child, and more importantly, the Prophet of God told you how your son was going to be tested and tried very early on because of the prophetic call and mandate on his life. He also told you to make sure that you do everything you can to put him around other prophetic people and introduce him to Bible early on in life.

    For the other mothers who are dealing with this similar problem with your child (ren) sleeping, I would like to suggest that you all make sure you anoint the room they sleep in with anointing oil. Make sure before they go to sleep to cover them in prayer and read Ephesians 6:13-17,

MERCEDES JOHNSON

this particular Scripture is the full armor of the Lord. You will want to make sure that you and your child pray this Scripture so that they can place upon themselves the full armor of God before they go to sleep. Amen.

And once again, I pray and release blessings over all of you, and I pray that you all were blessed, healed, delivered, and received revelation, insight, clarity and wisdom. God bless you all abundantly.

Love, Author of HerStory Breaking Through Darkness

HERSTORY BREAKING THROUGH DARKNESS

MERCEDES JOHNSON